The Global Messenger

MUHAMMAD

Peace be upon him

A Short Biography

**Compiled by
Umm Muhammad**

©**DAR ABUL-QASIM, 2016 (reprinted by GainPeace.com under license from the publisher, including title name and cover design changes, original details of which appear below)**

King Fahd National Library Cataloging-in-Publication Data

The Global Messenger
   The Global Messenger / Umm Muhammad – Jeddah, 2008
   102 p. 14 x 21 cm
   ISBN: 978-9960-887-28-9
   1 - Islam – General Principles   2 - Islamic Theology
   I - Title

                    Legal Deposit no. 1429/5589
                    ISBN: 978-9960-887-28-9

THIS BOOK HAS BEEN PRODUCED IN COLLABORATION WITH
ṢAḤEEḤ INTERNATIONAL™
Professional Editing and Typesetting of Islamic Literature

Table of Contents

FOREWORD

Advocates of secularism frequently blame religion for the unfortunate condition of our contemporary world[1] with the claim that it breeds fanaticism. Undoubtedly, violent acts committed by aggressive and irresponsible members of all major religions have increased substantially in recent years. Some of them are sanctioned internationally regardless of the issues at stake because misplaced sympathies and worldly interests so demand.

Our statement that Islam is a religion of peace and civilization might well be met with skepticism because this religion in particular has been the victim of its adherents as well as its enemies. Muslims long deprived of justice under the present world order are committing large scale criminal acts, erroneously assuming that the prolonged suffering of their peoples has earned them the right to take matters into their own hands. But in so doing they not only alienate public opinion but violate the most basic principles of their religion.[2]

Another cause for bleak impressions of Islam is an increasingly biased media portrayal that targets the religion rather than its errant followers.[3] In addition to the promotion of sensational misinformation, Islam's

---

[1] Disregarding how many have been killed by communists, nationalists and western nations who ignited two world wars within half a century, affecting half the population of the earth – not to speak of their current barbarism in various parts of the world.

[2] No matter how sorely oppressed, Muslims are prohibited from allowing emotion to govern their behavior, excusing it with naïve interpretations of their religious texts. As part of their commitment to God, they are under strict obligation to take their guidance from qualified scholars of Islamic jurisprudence regarding the interpretation of those texts and their application to critical contemporary situations.

[3] In addition, the legitimate defense of land, homes and citizens is inevitably labeled as terrorism when carried out by Muslims, while the state terrorism practiced by powerful nations against defenseless opponents is readily excused or even commended.

i

opponents have now perfected the art of provocation, aware that there is no shortage of Muslims whose frustration and anger will lead them to forget religious ethics and react impulsively. All that remains after that is for the media to capitalize on the regrettable errors committed. More recently, provocation has taken the form of deliberate slander and hostile attacks on the Prophet of Islam, enraging Muslims throughout the world to a degree that is difficult for an outsider to comprehend.

The positive side, however, is that Muslims have been belatedly prompted to correct the negative impressions and to share their noble Prophet with the world, something they should have been doing all along in view of the fact that he was sent with a global message for all mankind. The solution to ignorance and misunderstanding is education. Now, more than ever, Muslims need to answer to such questions as: "Who was Muhammad?" "Why is he loved so much by some and hated so much by others?" "Was he really a prophet of God?" "What did he teach?" "Did he live up to his claims?" "Did he encourage war and terrorism?" "What is the truth about this man?"

Non-Muslims, on the other hand, need to ask themselves honestly, "Does the religion itself encourage violence?" "Was this the teaching of Muhammad?" "Is everything we have been hearing lately the truth?" Then, they must seek answers with an open mind – from knowledgeable Muslims rather than biased western sources.

Religious conflicts are indeed a part of human history, but can strife be attributed to religion or to Islam in particular? Every prophet of God taught peaceful solutions through dialogue, appeal to reason, and opposition even to the worst tyranny with the least bloodshed possible. Enemies of those prophets, fearing loss of power and influence, perpetrated violence against them and their followers because they had no logical argument with which to save face and silence the opposition. And they, too, accused the advocates of religion of sedition and treason.

The purpose of this small book is not to answer ignorant or hostile critics, nor is it to recount praises of our Prophet as countless Muslim authors have done so eloquently over the centuries. Rather, it is to present facts that are based on historically verified sources and then leave the reader to make his own decision, or if he desires, to investigate the matter further.

The book is divided mainly into two sections, although the topics covered in both are interrelated and complimentary. The first acquaints the reader with information about the life of Prophet Muhammad and his global mission, while the second is concerned more with his teachings and way of life. All statements have been taken from authentic Arabic sources which are widely available for reference and study. But serious scholarship cannot rely on translations or compilations, such as this one, in languages other than the original. A work of this sort can be no more than an outline and is meant merely as an introduction to the Messenger of God and the message he was ordered to convey.

PART ONE

GENERAL INTRODUCTION

At the outset, a brief explanation of some basic terms can facilitate understanding of this book as well as other material related to Islam. This preface is limited to essential background information relevant to the book, while many other concepts, such as those of worship and *jihad,* should become clear within the content of the book.

Allah – One of the greatest misconceptions about Islam has to do with "*Allah,*" which some non-Muslims assume is a deity other than the God of the Jews and Christians. In the Arabic language, "Allah" is a proper name applicable only to the one true God who created and sustains the heavens and earth. It is the same name that all Arabic speaking people, regardless of their religion, use for the supreme being. In English, the difference between "God," meaning the one true God, and "god," meaning any false god, is a capital G. But in Arabic, "Allah" is a grammatically unique word which cannot be made plural or given a masculine or feminine gender. Therefore, it can never refer to a false god, and Muslims use the name "Allah" for God even when speaking other languages.

While Muslims, Christians, Jews and some others believe in the same God, their concepts of Him differ significantly. Muslims believe in one eternal, unique, absolute and perfect God who is the Creator and Sustainer of all that exists. Muslims acknowledge that He is the origin of all occurrences and that He alone is divine. His perfect attributes are unlike those of man or any other being and nothing resembles Him, so He cannot be compared to anything of His creation. He is in no way a part of His creation, nor is any of it a part of Him. The significance of this exclusive divinity is that no one and nothing in existence is worthy to be worshipped other than Allah, the one true God.

1

Islam – Monotheism is the essence of Islam, and it emphasizes the unity of divinity in contrast to the concept of trinity in Christianity and plurality of gods in other faiths. The meaning of "Islam" is peaceful submission; thus, it is a voluntary relationship between an individual and his Creator. And it is the only religion on earth which refuses the worship of any form of creation.

The Islamic creed did not begin with the prophethood of Muhammad, nor was it invented by him. It is basically the same message contained in previous divine scriptures and taught by all prophets of God. But because the earlier scriptures which taught the pure and correct belief in God were partially lost and altered through translations and human interference, Islam invites people to return to the true concept of God and to worship and obey Him alone.

Islamic beliefs are eternal truths that neither change nor develop, truths about God and His relationship with the visible and invisible aspects of the universe, about the reality of this life, about man's role therein, and what will become of him after it. The "pillars," or main requirements of faith, are belief in one God, in the angels created by Him, in the scriptures revealed by Him to His prophets, in the prophets through whom His revelation was conveyed to mankind, in the eternal life after death, and in God's perfect judgement and complete authority over human destiny.

Prophethood – Muslims believe in all the prophets and messengers sent by God. The Qur'an[4] states that prior to its revelation, at least one prophet or messenger had been sent at some time to every nation. Twenty-five of them are cited by name in the Qur'an, including some of those mentioned in the Old and New Testaments of the Bible. Most prominent among them are Noah, Abraham, Moses and Jesus. Every prophet was an outstanding

---

[4]The last revelation from God and His final message to mankind.

man in his community, both morally and intellectually. Each one stated clearly that what he conveyed was not from himself but an inspiration from God for the benefit of mankind. And each was supported by miracles granted by God as proof of his prophethood.

Prophets were human beings who, during particular periods of world development, conveyed a divine message to their peoples, supported by signs and miracles. All prophets were inspired with guidance, which they taught exactly as they were commanded. All were safeguarded by God from communicating any inaccuracies in the message, and they were protected from committing sins, with the exception of unintentional errors in worldly matters. All of them were truthful, intelligent, balanced and rational men. The slight differences in their teachings had to do with secondary aspects of legislation and procedures of worship, but all taught the worship of God alone and obedience to Him.

The last prophet and messenger sent to the world was named Muhammad bin Abdullah. He was a descendant of Prophet Ishmael, the son of Abraham,[5] and was from the Arab tribe of Quraysh. All good qualities and virtues were perfected in him even though he had not received any formal education or training. The revelation was brought to him by the angel Gabriel, also known to the Jews and Christians. The message he communicated, however, was not meant for any particular people, place, or period, but was a global message. The Messenger of Allah, as he was called, was appointed to instruct all of mankind and invite humanity to the same objective as did the prophets before him: the worship of God alone without associates or intermediaries.

His vision could not be attributed to the primitive, chaotic environment from which he came. It surpassed

---

[5]Isaac, another son of Abraham, was the ancestor of the Children of Israel, among whom a number of prophets were raised.

not only the limitations of that environment but those of many centuries to come. He taught that everyone has a vital duty to perform in the world at large. The final message conveyed to humanity by Prophet Muhammad and unchanged from the time of revelation sets right man's view of existence: the Creator and His creation, life and death, the present world and the Hereafter. It purifies religious belief from delusions of the mind and the excesses of imagination as well as from alteration based on human inclinations and opinions. This final message is distinguished by comprehensiveness, balance, universality, practicality and ease. It contains guidance for all of life and is for all peoples and all generations. Its rulings are precisely determined to benefit mankind and bring about material and spiritual elevation in both this life and the next.

Reverence for Prophet Muhammad in no way lessens that for the previous messengers, for all were sent to fulfill a purpose and all are held in high esteem by true believers. Muslims respect each of the prophets and messengers sent by God but are under obligation to follow the directives of Prophet Muhammad, since the revelation he conveyed contains the complete and final religion and legal code for humanity. Just as a newly revised law invalidates previous ones, the message revealed to the final prophet supersedes what came before it. It clarifies what had been obscured in previous scriptures and corrects the deviations that had gradually been introduced into pure monotheistic religion. Thus, there can be no legitimate claim to prophethood after Muhammad because his message is final and complete. He is quoted as having said, *"The Children of Israel were guided by prophets. When a prophet died, another succeeded him. However, there will be no prophet after me; only caliphs."*[6] And the Qur'an confirms the finality of his prophethood, stating that he is the "seal of the prophets."

---

[6]Narrated by al-Bukhari.

There is explicit evidence for the prophethood of Muhammad. His coming was foretold, and he was described in previous scriptures. The honest and open-minded among the Jews and Christians recognized him from those descriptions and believed in his message. As the revelation descended upon him, his companions noticed certain effects on his body; however, he never lost consciousness or showed any signs of illness. His life was protected by God during times of severe danger throughout the entire period of his prophethood until the divine message was complete. Like the prophets before him, Muhammad was supported with miracles; but by far the greatest of them was the Qur'an, an eternal miracle containing evidences for people of reason and understanding for all time to come.

Qur'an – The only divine scripture that has remained in the world completely intact up to the present day is the Qur'an.[7] It is God's ultimate and final message to mankind and the primary source of Islamic doctrine. It contains information and legislation which encompasses all spheres of human life.

There is only one version of the Qur'an, and unlike previous scriptures, it remains unaltered in its original Arabic text.[8] Initially, the revealed words were memorized by a large number of those who heard them directly from the Prophet. In addition, the entire revelation was recorded by several scribes during his lifetime, and its verses placed in the order he designated. Within a year after the Prophet's death, the written portions were collected and carefully checked against what had been memorized by his companions. Only that which was corroborated and witnessed was approved. The verified documents were then bound together, and from that volume a standard copy was later inscribed, rechecked, endorsed, reproduced

---

[7]Meaning literally: a "recitation" or "reading."

[8]Thus, it is easily accessible for study, as Arabic is a language used and understood by millions of people in the world today.

and distributed – all within less than fifteen years of the Prophet's demise. The Qur'an has been copied, printed, read, recited and memorized by millions of Muslims throughout the world up to the present day, and scholars have confirmed without a doubt that not the slightest change in content has occurred during its transmission from one generation to another.

The Qur'an states that this universe was not formed by chance, nor is it left to chance. God created it for a purpose and subjected it to physical laws for a specific period of time. Man was created for a purpose as well – to serve God upon the earth and live according to His law, which means the establishment of justice and attainment of practical solutions for human problems. The Qur'an does not condemn any religion directly; rather, it acknowledges the good works of previous religious communities but faults them for departing from the teachings of their prophets. It urges every religious person to search for the truth, to purify his belief, obey his Creator, and adhere to righteous conduct. It states that there is an ultimate consequence for every action, good and evil, and that there is a greater life following the present one in which complete justice will be realized for every human being, in fact, for every creature that ever existed.

The Qur'an is basically a book of guidance, but it does contain some amazing scientific facts. They are amazing because although they were revealed to Prophet Muhammad over 14 centuries ago, they were not really understood by man until scientists "discovered" them in recent times. In addition to religious and moral guidance it contains numerous verses that speak of the universe, its components and phenomena – the earth, sun, moon, stars, mountains, wind, rivers and seas, plants, animals, and successive stages of development of the human being. It appeals to logic, following clear reasoning and citing evidences from the created universe, from history and from the human soul, to establish not only the

6

existence of God but also His uniqueness and absolute perfection.

Muhammad and the Qur'an – Opponents of Islam sometimes allege that Muhammad himself wrote the Qur'an or that he copied or adapted it from previous scriptures.[9] But it is known that the Prophet's contacts with Jews and Christians was negligible before his emigration from Makkah, and after it, his role was that of a teacher, openly inviting the Jews and Christians to accept Islam while pointing out how they had deviated from the true monotheism taught by their prophets.

Historically and logically, it cannot be established that there was any human source for the Qur'an or that the Messenger of Allah learned it from the Jews or Christians. His enemies kept a close watch on him hoping to find confirmation of their claim that he was a liar. But they could not point to a single instance when the Prophet might have had secret meetings with people of other faiths.

At the time the Qur'an was revealed, his contemporaries among the Arabs (who were renowned for linguistic eloquence) acknowledged that its language was unique and distinctly different from the speech of Muhammad, a man well known to them. The Qur'an states that the Prophet was an unlettered man, so if that had not been true, his opponents would surely have exposed him. There is, however, not a single report to this effect, and no one denied his illiteracy. At the same time, no one

---

[9]It is true that there are some similarities between the Qur'an and the Bible, but this does not indicate that later prophets plagiarized from former ones. It merely points to the common source, which is the Creator of mankind, and to the continuance of His basic message of monotheism. Moreover, there was no Arabic version of the Bible in existence at the time of Prophet Muhammad. The earliest Arabic version of the Old Testament is that of R. Saadias Gaon of 900 CE – more than 250 years after the death of Prophet Muhammad. And the oldest Arabic version of the New Testament was published by Erpenius in 1616 CE – about 1,000 years after his death.

denied that the Qur'an was unequaled in eloquence, impact and clarity, including those who rejected its message.

It was a sign of Muhammad's prophethood that he was an illiterate man. He had to be, so that he could never be accused of composing or editing the divine revelations. This fact also eliminates suspicion that he had learned what he preached from earlier scriptures. The information he passed to his people was not obtained through reading and research; it was a kind of knowledge that could only have come from the Creator of the universe.[10]

It is not difficult to verify that Muhammad did not possess knowledge of many things mentioned in the Qur'an, such as historical events, natural phenomena and future occurrences. The Qur'an even states in several places that Muhammad and his people did not know these facts, so again, had it been otherwise, his adversaries would have capitalized on that claim to discredit him. Only recently, within the last two centuries, have advancements in research technology led to the discovery of facts that had been mentioned in the Qur'an by the unlettered prophet over fourteen centuries ago. Among them are these few examples:

- The creation of the universe from a single entity and of life from water: **"Have those who disbelieved not considered that the heavens and the earth were a joined entity, and We separated them and made from water every living thing?"**[11]

- All creation is based on duality, made up of pairs, counterparts or opposites: **"And of all things We created two mates."**[12]

---

[10]In addition, the Qur'an, on occasion, reproaches the Prophet and brings his attention to some unintentional errors. It is quite unlikely that he would have included such criticisms of himself had he been its author.

[11]Qur'an, 21:30.

[12]Qur'an, 51:49. In contrast, the Creator is one, with no counterpart and nothing resembling Him in any way.

- The different natures of the sun and moon: **"It is He [the Creator] who made the sun a shining light and the moon a derived light and determined for it phases – that you may know the number of years and account [of time]."**[13]
- The rotation of the earth: **"He created the heavens and earth in truth. He wraps the night over the day and wraps the day over the night."**[14]
- The expansion of the universe: **"And the heaven We constructed with strength, and indeed, We are [its] expander."**[15]
- The sun is not stationary but moves in a specific direction for a limited term: **"And the sun runs [on course] toward its stopping point."**[16]

These are words that were recited by Muhammad, the unlettered prophet. Nothing mentioned in the Qur'an contradicts any established scientific fact, and it addresses these facts with the precision of a scientist. Could the most highly literate, well read or scholarly man of that period, or even of the centuries that followed, possibly have come up with anything remotely similar? The answer is obvious.

Although not meant to be a book of scientific facts as such, the Qur'an mentions certain realities that would only be recognized and appreciated by men in later centuries – as undeniable evidence that it was not the work of Muhammad or of any man but divine revelation

---

[13]Qur'an, 10:5. Other verses (25:61 and 71:16) refer to the sun as a burning lamp.

[14]Qur'an, 39:5. The alternate "wrapping" of sunlight and darkness is caused by the earth's turning in one direction.

[15]Qur'an, 51:47. The Creator refers to Himself in the plural form which denotes power, grandeur and majesty.

[16]Qur'an, 36:38. The sun, as a tiny member of this vast universe, is progressing within it toward a final destination, which indicates an end to the present creation.

from the Creator of these phenomena. Being the final revelation to mankind, God made the Qur'an a continuing miracle containing evidences to be uncovered gradually as men increase in knowledge of their universe.

Hadith – The teachings of Prophet Muhammad, apart from the text of the Qur'an, are also available today and contained in verified records. His sayings, actions and reactions in every situation throughout his life were related and recorded by those who actually witnessed or heard them. A narration of this kind is called a *hadith.* Every *hadith* has two parts: the text and the list of transmitters. Even when the text seems correct and logical, it must be supported by an unbroken chain of reliable reporters going back directly to the Prophet himself in order to be accepted by jurists. Scholars carefully scrutinize the reliability of the transmitters, accepting only those *hadiths* whose chain of narrators is known to be completely reliable and sound. When verified as authentic, these narrations become a supplement to the Qur'an as the basic foundation of Islamic legislation.

The science of *hadith* criticism began at an early date. The Prophet's companions learned and passed on his teachings by three methods: memorization, written records and practice. They not only memorized and recorded the revelations which made up the Qur'an, but also committed to memory the exact words used by the Prophet in his own statements as well as descriptions of his behavior and character. After his death, as Islam was spread by the companions into Asia and North Africa, this knowledge accompanied them, and their students faithfully preserved it for following generations.

As the narrations were subsequently conveyed from teacher to student, it is a credit to their scholarship that the narrations were always preceded by a list of narrators going back to the Prophet himself. This enabled later scholars to check out each narration and reject it if the chain of narrators contained anyone who was unknown or was known to be weak in memory or prone to error. Only those narrations whose chains were complete and whose transmitters were unblemished could actually be attributed to the Prophet and accepted as authoritative.

This kind of scholarship became all the more essential in later years when some Muslims began to forge *hadiths* to support their own views and spread them among the common people. Although they succeeded in their deception for a time, the false narrations were eventually exposed by *hadith* specialists. Their strict and precise methodology enables us today to know which *hadiths* are authentic and which ones are weak and unacceptable as evidence. The great body of information so conscientiously collected and thoroughly analyzed for accuracy by Muslim scholars now fills hundreds of volumes, not to mention the studies which have developed around it.

Biography – Along with the large collection of *hadiths,* the biography (*seerah*) of Prophet Muhammad is well known as a part of recorded history. However, there is a subtle difference between *hadith* literature and the Prophet's biography. His biographers were historians who, within the first century after his death, began to gather all the facts they could from the various sources available. These included descriptions of battles and other events, descriptions of the Prophet's character, descriptions of people with whom he came in contact, and various other biographical information. The early biographers had all they could manage to collect and record the abundant amount of material, and they expected that others would assume the task of confirming its authenticity. Thus, many of their statements began with the words, "It was said" or "They claimed," showing that the information had not yet been systematically verified. This is an expression of integrity seldom found among conventional historians.

Unfortunately, due to pressing matters of the time, research into the narrations was delayed, meaning that the biographies remained more or less on a par with other history books; yet they were in accord with one another on all major events and occurrences. Within the last century there has been renewed effort by a number of Muslim scholars to sift through this material, discard what is unconfirmed and retain that which can be verified. For this purpose they often refer the information to scholars of *hadith,* whose methodology is based on strict rules and defined principles. In this way, every statement given by a biographer can be evaluated.

TRANSPARENT PERSONALITY

Throughout its history the world has produced countless illustrious individuals. But as a rule they were figures who distinguished themselves in limited areas, such as political or military leadership. The stories of earlier prophets have become so polluted with fiction that an accurate and authentic account of their lives is no longer available. But this is not the case with Prophet Muhammad, who accomplished so much in so many diverse fields. Every detail of his private life and public speech has been documented and carefully preserved up to the present day. In fact, no biography of any human being has been preserved as well as his.

The Prophet's personality was noble and balanced, and his lifestyle was all-encompassing. Within his sayings and his biography can be found that which concerns and relates to all people at all times: in ease or hardship, peace or war, victory or defeat. And within them can be found every feature of his character, for example:

The devout worshipper – His greatest pleasure was in prayer, for that is when a believer is closest to his Lord. He would stand in prayer at night so long that his feet would swell, and he would weep until his beard was wet. He used to fast often, usually on specific days of the week and month. He was constantly aware of his Lord, remembering Him in every situation and fearing His displeasure. He constantly sought forgiveness for his human errors and confided, *"Indeed, I repent to Allah a hundred times daily."*[17] His praises and supplications reflected the highest degree of sincerity and servitude and the highest aspirations one can have for himself and others.

He was indifferent to worldly things and content with little, even though he was eventually granted victories, war booty and sovereignty over the Arabian peninsula. He did not refuse the good things of life when they were available and would be grateful for them. But when they were not available, he would not seek them out or regret the shortage. He would live mostly on dates and water, and often months passed when no fire was lit for cooking in his house. He slept on a simple straw mat and said, *"What do I need of this world? It is like the shade of a tree in which a rider naps at noon; then he moves on and leaves it."*[18]

But while the Prophet encouraged people to perform acts of worship, he warned them against going to extremes in the practice of religion. He disapproved of taking on acts of voluntary worship beyond what could be done with ease, in order to prevent enthusiastic believers from neglecting other responsibilities or from exhausting themselves physically or spiritually. Rather, he taught moderation in this respect and that small works done regularly earn more reward in the long run than a great amount done for awhile and later abandoned.

Member of a family and community – Despite his extraordinary spirituality and indifference to the world, he was not heedless of central aspects of life, nor did he neglect its duties and responsibilities. He did not forget

---

[17]Narrated by Ahmad and Muslim.
[18]Narrated by Ahmad and at-Tirmidhi.

that he was a husband, father, grandfather, relative, neighbor, friend and leader, and that each of these has obligations toward others. He was a human being, one that could be pleased, angry, happy or sad. He would joke with his companions at times, yet not speak except the truth. When he was angry, it did not prevent him from justice and morality; and when he was saddened, he bore it with patience and acceptance.

He was a husband who, despite of his great concerns and responsibilities, was fair and just with his wives,[19] pleasing them as much as possible, settling problems among them, considering their feelings, and appreciating the individuality and circumstances of each one. Among his wives were those who were young and old, a daughter of his sworn enemy, and a daughter of his closest friend. They represented the spectrum of society. One was occupied with raising orphans, another was characterized by fasting and praying a great deal at night, and several were known for scholarship. He sought good marriages for his daughters and was an affectionate father to his children and grandchildren. He was concerned with the rights of relatives, including the non-Muslims among them. He was loyal to his friends and companions and observed the rights of neighbors, even those who were insensitive and abusive.

Head of state, teacher and advisor – He became the head of an emerging state surrounded on all sides by enemies. He established political ties with the various factions among the local inhabitants and drew up a constitution. He received delegations and sent messages. He knew that man has a responsibility to develop the earth and civilize it, and was a perfect example of balance

---

[19]It is noteworthy that in a world which had previously allowed men an unlimited number of wives, it was Islam that came to regulate the practice by limiting the number of wives to four and establishing the condition of fair treatment for each. But, for reasons known to God, the prophets were not restricted to four wives as are Muslims in general.

and moderation. He developed a well-disciplined nation out of chaotic tribalism and provided peace in place of war. He advised people to spend within their means, neither to be so excessive as to make themselves insolvent, nor to withhold from those in need. It is said that morals are known during power and predominance. When the Prophet enjoyed power and influence, he demonstrated the highest level of morality, even toward those who opposed him in combat.

Commander of the army – Prophet Muhammad's message was primarily one of mercy, but he was obliged to turn to battle when certain powers refused mercy and morality and sought to deprive others of them and of their natural rights and individual freedoms. He was a commander who gathered statistics about military capabilities, sent scouts to gather information, and drew up battle plans. Aware that the Creator had ordained for every occurrence a cause, he applied this natural law in order to achieve success. He made full use of all means available, applied strategies and called upon his Lord for assistance. After that he could expect divine support, knowing that he had fulfilled his obligation.

The total number of days the Prophet was required to spend in defensive warfare comes to less than a year. His most famous battles did not last for more than one day, and the total number of the enemy slain during battle has been recorded at 759. With very few exceptions, enemy captives and the wounded were treated with benevolence and justice.[20] After the conquest of Makkah there were no reprisals. Only four of the enemy were executed, and that was due to their previous crimes rather than to the fact that they were captives.

Muhammad was no more than a human being, but he was a man with a noble mission. During the 23-year

---

[20]When a few zealous Muslims transgressed on occasion, they were severely rebuked.

period of his prophethood, he changed the entire Arabian Peninsula from paganism to worship of the one true God, from tribal wars to national unity, from anarchy to disciplined living, from barbarism to the highest standards of moral excellence. No other man in history excelled in so many different aspects of life. He not only taught and established the religion but founded a state, initiated numerous political and social reforms, built a powerful and dynamic society, and completely revolutionized the realm of human thought and behavior – all within just over two decades.

Some have asserted that the message he brought was a product of his own mind. But if that was so, why did he not take credit for it? He could have claimed supernatural qualities, enjoyed recognition, accepted a high position of leadership, or at least avoided adversity and opposition. But Muhammad maintained the opposite: that he was a human being like everyone else, that he spoke nothing of his own accord, and that the Qur'an, the like of which humanity could not produce, was a message from God revealed to him by God, to whom alone belongs all glory and praise. All of the legislation he pronounced, the principles he taught, and the great achievements for which he could have attained personal renown and advantage were attributed to the guidance and support of God alone. At the time of his death, in spite of his nation's increasing material wealth, he possessed nothing of worldly value. His character, generosity, righteousness and integrity all stand as irrefutable evidence of his prophethood.

While it was still in its early stages, the Qur'an disclosed that Islam was indeed a global religion. Allah addressed His Prophet therein, saying: **"And We have not sent you but as a mercy to [all] the worlds."**[21] **"And We have not sent you except comprehensively to mankind, as a bringer**

---

[21]Qur'an, 21:107.

of good tidings and a warner, but most of the people do not know."[22]

Islam is meant for all people regardless of race, nationality, cultural or religious background. The Prophet and his followers made every effort to spread the message of truth to all nations and peoples. From the commencement of his mission, his companions came from a wide range of lands and races. Among them was Bilal, an African; Suhaib, a Byzantine; Salman, a Persian and Ibn Salam, a Jewish scholar. All were united in the brotherhood of faith.[23]

As the Prophet undertook to follow and teach the directives that came to him through the divine revelation, great changes came about in peoples who would otherwise have been unnoticed by history. But the resulting historical events are, in themselves, given less importance by Muslim scholars than the human factor that caused them – the direct relationship between the positive attitudes and efforts of men and the result bestowed upon them by God in the form of success and blessing in this worldly life, even before that of the Hereafter.

SUMMARY OF EVENTS

Before Prophethood – Prophet Muhammad was born to the tribe of Quraysh in the Arabian city of Makkah. This city had been built up around the *Ka'bah,* the structure built by Prophets Abraham and Ishmael in response to a divine command. The two prophets, to whom Muhammad's ancestry is traced, had dedicated the House for the worship of Allah, the one true God.

---

[22]Qur'an, 34:28.

[23]The modern Muslim world, from Asia to Africa and into Europe is further proof that Islam is a universal message for all mankind – not to mention the fact that significant numbers of western Europeans and Americans of all races and ethnic backgrounds are discovering and entering Islam.

17

But with the passing of centuries, the tribes of Arabia, while still acknowledging Allah as the Creator, had turned to polytheism and idol worship. Some claimed that these idols were intermediaries between the people and Allah, while others worshipped Allah as merely one of their many deities. They had filled and surrounded the *Ka'bah* with statues, stones and other objects of worship.

The House of Allah was what made Makkah a center of commerce as well as one of worship and gave its people honor among the neighboring tribes. During the pilgrimage season in particular, the Quraysh hosted guests and delegations from near and far. As custodians of the *Ka'bah,* they were guardians of the idols as well. Their prestige and authority throughout the Arabian peninsula and beyond was derived from this role, and their business interests necessitated the maintenance of this tradition.

A year before the birth of the Prophet, a Christian army commanded by Abrahah al-Ashram, a ruler of Yemen, marched to the outskirts of Makkah with the intention of destroying the *Ka'bah*. He had hoped to replace the *Ka'bah,* the center of worship and pilgrimage for the Arabs, with a large cathedral he had built in Sanaa. His army of 60,000 men included a number of elephants. The army advanced unopposed until it reached the outskirts of Makkah, and the Quraysh, powerless to resist, could only hide in the nearby mountains and wait. Defenseless and in desperation, they began to supplicate Allah fervently to protect His House.

The way was clear for the army, led by one huge elephant, to enter the city and attack the *Ka'bah,* but Allah willed otherwise. Every time they urged the elephant toward Makkah, it refused to advance. They beat and slashed it with irons, but to no avail. When turned in the opposite direction, it would take off; but when faced toward Makkah, it would kneel and refuse to move. This went on until there appeared in the sky great flocks of birds carrying stones in their beaks and claws. These stones they released on the army, tearing their skins and infecting them with disease. Many of the aggressors perished on the spot, and others, including Abrahah, fled in panic and died on the way back.

During a period of difficulty at the outset of his prophethood, Allah consoled His Messenger with the following verses from the Qur'an: **"Have you not considered how your Lord dealt with the companions of the elephant? Did He not make their plan into misguidance? And He sent against them birds in flocks, striking them with stones of hard clay. And He made them like chewed up straw."**[24] It was a reminder of how Allah had protected His House from harm, while the polytheists and their idols were helpless to do so. Prophet Muhammad would also be protected by Allah until his mission was complete. He was born later in that same year, which was known to the tribes as "the Year of the Elephant."

Although Allah was still acknowledged in name, the people of Arabia had all but forgotten the religion of their forefathers, Abraham and Ishmael. They were steeped in immoralities and injustices of every kind and often occupied by bloody tribal feuds. Except for idol worship and some traditional sentiments of Arab chivalry, they had no common objective or code of ethics to guide their conduct. They were a people plunged in ignorance, in gambling and intoxication, devotion to idols and committing abominations. They mistreated their neighbors, buried their female children alive, and as a rule, the strong devoured the weak. It was into this corrupt and tradition centered society that the Messenger of Allah was born.

Muhammad grew up as an orphan, as his father, Abdullah, had died before his birth, and his mother,

---

24Qur'an, 105:1-5.

Aminah, passed away when he was yet six years old. His grandfather, Abdul-Muttalib, who had taken the boy following the death of his mother, himself died two years later, and the guardianship then went to his son, Abu Talib, who was an honorable but very poor man. Muhammad was raised by his uncle with love and care within his meager circumstances. As a boy, Prophet Muhammad tended sheep and later made a living through trade and commerce.

When Muhammad was nine years old, he insisted on accompanying Abu Talib on a journey to Syria in a merchant caravan. As the caravan reached the town of Busra, it halted for a short rest, and there they met a Christian monk by the name of Baheera. He came out of his cell to welcome the merchants and prepared a meal for them. The caravan had attracted Baheera because of something he had observed from a distance. When the monk saw the boy, he noticed the signs of prophethood that he had learned from the scriptures. He advised Abu Talib to return the youth to his home and guard him from the Jews, adding that great honor awaited his nephew. Abu Talib immediately sent Muhammad back to Makkah.

Muhammad had no formal education, but his intelligence, honesty and sincerity made him widely respected as a young man. Allah had developed his mind and kept him away from the negative aspects of pagan society. Since early youth, he was known for moderation, integrity and a serious sense of responsibility. His upright nature won him the title of "al-Ameen," which means "the Trustworthy." He was skilled in public relations and during reparation of the *Ka'bah* managed to avert a major crisis among the quarrelling tribes. His sense of justice also prompted him to encourage and participate in the drawing up of a pact[25] among the Makkans for the protection of weaker members of society

---

25Called "Hilful-Fudul."

from exploitation and oppression by the powerful. The high moral character of such a man within a corrupt society attests to the divine will in preparing him for the prophethood.

At the age of twenty-five, he married Khadijah, a noble widow of forty. She was a businesswoman, and like other merchants of Makkah, she would hire men to transport her goods and engage in trade on her behalf. Having heard of Muhammad's integrity, she employed him to accompany her merchandise to Syria. She was pleased with the profits he brought her and greatly impressed with his character. She sent someone to propose marriage to him in spite of having previously refused many wealthy and influential suitors. Muhammad remained contentedly married to Khadijah until her death, twenty-five years later. She bore him two sons, who died in early childhood, and four daughters, all of whom embraced Islam as adults.

Although the marriage freed him from financial need, Muhammad had little interest in worldly affairs. He had always had an instinctive aversion to the traditional idol worship of his society, and in the period following his marriage, he turned increasingly to contemplation, longing to know more about the religion of his ancestor, the prophet Abraham, and the truth about Allah. He himself neither sought prophethood nor had it ever occurred to him. But the spiritual unrest and dissatisfaction he felt with the way of life observed around him led him to seek seclusion in order to contemplate and worship Allah in his own way. He began to retire to the cave of Hiraa' in a mountain far outside the city for meditation and prayer. Unaware of what this internal disquiet meant, the thought that he was about to be honored with prophethood never crossed his mind.

The Makkan Period – The first signs of prophethood came in the form of dreams, which inevitably came true shortly after their occurrence. Then, at the age of forty, while he was alone as usual in the cave, the angel Gabriel[26] appeared before him, commanding him to recite. Muhammad replied truthfully, "I am not one who can recite." He had never indulged in the recitation of poetry, a favorite pastime of his contemporaries among the Arabs. The Prophet related that the angel pressed him forcefully, after which he released him and said again, "Recite."[27] He replied a second time, "I am not one who can recite." The angel again pressed him as before and on releasing him said, "Recite." When Muhammad replied once again that he could not recite, the angel pressed him even more forcefully in the same manner. He then released him and delivered the first of the revelations from Allah which he was to receive in portions over a period of twenty-three years:

"Recite in the name of your Lord who created –
Created man from a clinging clot.
Recite, and your Lord is most generous,
Who taught by the pen –
Taught man that which he knew not."[28]

The Prophet recited these verses and the angel departed. This event took place in the middle of the lunar month of Ramadhan in the year 610 CE. Terrified at what he had experienced, Muhammad fled to the comfort of his wife, Khadijah, who reassured him that because of his kindness, generosity and righteousness, Allah would never harm him. She was the first to believe in his prophethood. She then took him to her aged cousin, Waraqah bin Nawfal, who had become a Christian and had knowledge of the earlier scriptures. When he heard about the extraordinary occurrence, he realized that

---

[26]Arabic: Jibreel.

[27]The word "*iqra*" can be translated as either "recite" or "read." Some commentators prefer the latter as it is known that the Prophet was illiterate.

[28]Qur'an, 96:1-5.

Muhammad was the long awaited Prophet of God. He said, "That is the angel Allah sent to Moses. If only I was younger and could be alive when your people drive you out." "Will they drive me out?" asked Muhammad. "Yes," replied Waraqah, "For no man has ever come with anything like what You have brought but that he was harmed. If I should live to see that day, I will support you vigorously." But he died shortly afterward.

After the initial revelation there was a period of pause. Commentators suggest that the interruption was in order to allow the fear in the Prophet's heart to subside. There are reports to the effect that after that first experience, he doubted his sanity and considered throwing himself from the peak of a mountain. But the angel Gabriel would appear to him, saying, "Muhammad, you are truly the Messenger of Allah."[29]

Once his anxiety had diminished, Muhammad began to await return of the revelation and then even to long for it. He related to his companions how it resumed: *"While I was walking, I heard a voice from the heaven. I lifted my head and there was the angel that had come to me in Hiraa', seated on a chair between the heaven and earth. I was terrified of him and returned home. I told them, 'Wrap me up! Wrap me up!' so they wrapped me [in garments]. But then Allah, the Exalted, sent down the words:* **'O you who covers himself, arise and warn. And your Lord glorify, and your clothing purify, and contamination avoid.'** *After that the revelation began to come more frequently and in succession."*[30]

These preliminary instructions were given to the Prophet at the commencement of his mission. He was told what to do and what kind of life to adopt. He was to

---

29Narrated by al-Bukhari.

30Narrated by al-Bukhari. The Qur'anic verses quoted are 74:1-5. "Contamination" here refers to spiritual as well as physical impurity and alludes to polytheism and idol worship.

forsake the comforts of ordinary life, dedicate himself to Allah, and arise to the awesome task ahead of him. From that moment on, Prophet Muhammad's life was never to be the same; it would be a continuous struggle to fulfill the trust placed upon him by his Lord.

The message he was to impart was that of every prophet before him: that there is nothing worthy of worship and obedience except the Mighty and Majestic God who created this universe and maintains everything in existence. The Prophet was ordered to issue a warning, which meant ignorance could no longer be justification for wrongdoing, and that those warned would be held fully accountable for their actions. He invited people to belief in Allah as their true God, their Creator and Sustainer, and to believe in resurrection after death, the final account, and just recompense in an eternal life. This religion, called "Islam," meant submission to the will of God by all people, without any distinction between them. It was a universal call – all believers were to be brothers and equals.

The Messenger of Allah began with discretion by imparting the message privately to those close to him who knew him best and trusted him most. The first Muslim believer was Khadijah, followed by Zayd, a slave boy he had freed and adopted as a son, and his young cousin Ali, who had also been raised in his home. Next was his closest friend Abu Bakr, through whose efforts a number of others were convinced of the truth of Islam. These enthusiastic forerunners of the religion soon became over forty in number. The word began to spread within the city that Muhammad was teaching some sort of new faith. The number of Muslims continued to increase to the point that curiosity was aroused among the people of Makkah. But most of them were yet unconcerned and continued to view the Prophet and his followers with indifference.

24

He would meet with them and teach them regularly as more and more verses of the Qur'an were revealed in a fascinating and powerful language. The lives of these men and women were completely transformed, and they became examples of the highest degree of virtue and courage. The group of early believers also shared a strong bond of brotherhood based on the new consciousness of Allah and their common effort to spread and teach His religion and way of life. Within three years the faith was firmly established in the hearts of the Prophet's companions, and the period of individual propagation was drawing to a close.

Through the Qur'an, Allah then ordered His Messenger to take the message to the public, saying: **"And warn your closest kindred."**[31] This was a reference to his tribe, the Quraysh, who inhabited Makkah and the surrounding areas, but it was also an order to make himself known to all peoples of the world. Given the tribal mentality of the Makkans, it was not only natural but prudent to begin public propagation with his closest kindred, for they were the ones who would be most likely to support him or at least defend him as their sense of honor prescribed. It did not mean, however, that the message was restricted to the Quraysh, but only that informing them was a logical first step toward the realization of a long term goal. It was clear from many verses revealed, even early ones, that the Prophet's mission was to be a global one. Several of them which mention the revelation conclude with: **"And it is not but a reminder for the worlds."**

After issuing a number of invitations in which he explained the religion and expressed concern for the people's destiny, the Prophet issued an alarm call, mounted the hill of Safa near the *Ka'bah,* and addressed the crowd that had gathered: "If I was to inform you that horsemen were in the valley behind this hill ready to

---

[31]Qur'an, 26:214.

attack you, would you believe me?" The question was meant to obtain their confirmation of his honesty, credibility and reliability. They replied, "Yes, for we have never known you to lie." Having gained their vote of confidence, he continued, "Indeed, I am a warner to you of a severe punishment." Another uncle of the Prophet, Abu Lahab, replied, "May you be ruined for the rest of the day. Is this what you gathered us for?" And he got up and left.[32]

The Prophet of Allah continued to address the Quraysh in obedience to the command of his Lord: **"And say, 'Indeed, I am the clear warner.'"**[33] He would invite them to the mercy of Allah and warn them to save themselves from the Hellfire, adding that his kinship would not benefit them before Allah at all, due to the fact that every individual is accountable for his deeds. His concern for them was evident in the sadness he felt upon their rejection of his message, and he increased his efforts to speak whenever the opportunity arose.

The Qur'anic revelation came frequently with vivid descriptions of Paradise and Hellfire, with encouragement and warning to all those it was to reach. Allah's Messenger instructed his followers to learn the verses by heart and those who were skilled in writing to record them as soon as he recited them. Like his predecessors among the prophets, he lived and taught total commitment to the conviction that Allah, the Creator, was to be worshipped alone, without equals or associates. He firmly rejected the worship of any created being and was saddened by the degradation of humanity resulting from such practices.

The revelations that came to the Prophet during the Makkan period dealt mainly with matters of belief – the unity and exclusiveness of Allah, His absolute power and

---

[32]Thereupon a short chapter of the Qur'an was revealed, which begins: **"May the hands of Abu Lahab be ruined, and ruined is he."** (111:1)
[33]Qur'an, 15:89.

ability, and His mercy. It informed of the Judgement, the rewards and punishments of the Hereafter, and the personal responsibility of every soul. It taught morality, piety, patience, the spirit of sacrifice, and dependence upon Allah. It comforted the believers in hardship, giving examples of the difficulties faced by the earlier prophets in their struggle to re-establish the worship of Allah on earth. And finally, it reassured them that Allah in His wisdom always does what is best. The early chapters came in powerful language aimed at awakening the hearts of men who had long been unaware.

As a rule, any new concept on the rise in society will be met with a certain apprehensiveness, skepticism and often, disapproval and opposition. The wider the disparity between the traditional beliefs and customs and the newly proposed ideals, the greater the discord between the two. The message Muhammad brought, calling on people to reject false deities – stones, idols or anything else – and to worship Allah exclusively, was in clear contrast to the ways of those who were satisfied with their erroneous beliefs, irrational customs and moral corruption. The worship of Allah alone was clearly understood by all the Arabs to mean full obedience to the legislation he was sending down, not only in regard to religious rites, but in the establishment of comprehensive moral principles based on justice and benefit for all. For those in power it would mean some concession of authority and limitation of worldly advantages; hence the majority of them refused it outright.

Despite increasing problems, the Prophet never ceased to seek out and speak to any who would listen. The polytheistic traditionalists perceived a threat to their established way of life and to the authority which was derived from that social order. The reaction among the Quraysh in Makkah was first ridicule and then persecution of the growing group of Muslims. The Prophet was then directed: **"So declare what you are commanded and turn**

away from the polytheists."[34]   By so doing, believers would now be irrefutably distinguished from non-believers both in their creed and in their conduct.   The declaration ordered by Allah was no less than an exposure of the ineffectiveness of idolatry and superstition supported by clear proofs and indications.

Unable to deal with such pronouncements coming from the man they had always referred to as "the Trustworthy," the Quraysh convened and called upon the Prophet's uncle and guardian, Abu Talib, to convince his nephew to cease these menacing activities.   But Abu Talib, while advising him, continued to treat Muhammad benevolently and to protect him.   Nothing could persuade him to abandon the nephew he loved like his own sons.   Impatient to end the disruption of their established social order, the influential chiefs of Makkah attempted to dissuade the Prophet by offering him wealth and authority in return for the abandonment of his call to worship one God and the criticism of their traditions, in particular, idol worship.

Finally, they gave Abu Talib an ultimatum: he must either prevent his nephew from speaking out or allow them to deal with him themselves.   But even if his uncle should no longer be willing to shield him, the Messenger of Allah had no option but to continue in his mission.   He told him, "O uncle, by Allah, if they were to place the sun in my right hand and the moon in my left for me to give up this matter, I would not give it up until Allah makes it successful or else I perish in the effort."   Abu Talib could only say, "Go where you will and say what you will.   By Allah, I will never deliver you to your enemies."

Criticism of traditions long held sacred and open denunciation of paganism generated intense enmity among those firmly attached to their ancestral beliefs. Their resentment provoked them to violence against weak members of the society who had accepted Islam.   The

---

[34]Qur'an, 5:94.

leaders of Quraysh persuaded other tribes to take similar measures against the defenseless and vulnerable Muslims among them. The attitude of the Quraysh strongly influenced other Arabs who respected them as caretakers of the *Ka'bah.* Many believers were compelled to endure beatings, shackles and imprisonment with denial of food and water. Some were stretched on burning sands with heavy rocks placed on their chests, and some were burned with red hot irons. Several died as a result of torture, but not one would renounce his faith.

All attempts to seduce the companions away from Islam had ended in failure, as did their efforts to stop the Prophet from preaching the religion so fearlessly. As the hostility of the persecutors increased, so did the number of the Prophet's followers. The polytheistic establishment then decided that people visiting Makkah had to be kept away from the Prophet lest they hear his words and be convinced by them. They lashed out against him personally, calling him a liar, a sorcerer and a poet. They insulted, harassed and abused him in every manner, disregarding the traditional ties of kinship and all humanitarian concerns.

Persecution increased to an alarming degree, but the Prophet restrained his followers from striking back and counseled patience and forbearance in the face of hardship until such a time as Allah would show them the way. Complete trust in the divine promise and compensation of the Hereafter disciplined the Muslims and strengthened their will. Finally, in the fifth year of prophethood, Allah's Messenger gave permission for his followers to seek refuge in Abyssinia, where they were received sympathetically by the Negus, a Christian king who proved to be just and benevolent. It was there the Muslims found an agreeable environment where they could reside until the situation at home improved. A total of eighty-three persons are reported to have migrated to Abyssinia, some alone and others accompanied by their families.

The news that Muslims had found peace in Abyssinia reached Makkah, making the pagan establishment all the more angry and frustrated. Their agents soon arrived at the king's court bearing gifts and requesting surrender of the refugees. But the Negus deemed it highly improper to hand over those who had sought his asylum. When the envoys of the Quraysh persisted in their demand, presenting him with a negative portrayal of the religion they professed, he summoned the Muslims to his court in the presence of his bishops and asked: "What is this religion for which you have forsaken your people?"

Ja'far, a son of Abu Talib and cousin of the Prophet, arose on behalf of the Muslims and addressed the ruler, saying, "O King, we were a people absorbed in ignorance. We worshipped idols, ate dead animals, committed immoralities, broke ties of relationship, mistreated our neighbors and exploited the weak. But then God sent a prophet from among us whose honesty, truthfulness and trustworthiness we knew. He invited us to acknowledge the oneness of God, to worship Him alone, and to renounce the stones and idols we and our forefathers used to worship. He enjoined us to speak the truth, to fulfill our trusts, and to observe the rights of our relatives and neighbors. He ordered us to refrain from everything unlawful and from bloodshed. He forbade us from immoralities, telling lies, taking the property of orphans, and from speaking ill of chaste women. He ordered us to worship God alone, without any associate, to perform prayer, give the poor-due and observe fasting. We believed in him and followed him in what he brought us from the religion of God, so we worshipped God alone without associating anything with Him. We considered unlawful what he prohibited and accepted what he permitted. Hence, our people made enemies of us and tormented us; they tried to prevent us from our faith and return us to the worship of idols after we had worshipped God, and return us to unlawful practices. So when they oppressed, tortured, restricted and prevented us from the practice of our religion, we fled to your country, having chosen you over all others. We have come seeking your protection and expect we will not be treated unjustly with you, O King."

The Negus listened carefully to the words of Ja'far, who had spoken truthfully and frankly, well aware that Christian beliefs differed somewhat from those he had expressed. He knew that his words could affect the outcome of this critical meeting. The king inquired of Ja'far if he could recite anything that had been conveyed from God to his prophet, so he recited from the Qur'an the opening verses of the chapter called *Maryam*, in which Allah describes the birth of Prophet John and the virgin birth of Prophet Jesus to Mary. The Negus wept as did his bishops. He exclaimed, "Indeed, this [recitation] and that which Jesus brought came from a single [source of] light." And he granted asylum to the Muslims.

The departure of Muslims from Makkah resulted in additional persecution for those who remained behind. Frustration at their failure to stop them led the Quraysh to increase pressure on Abu Talib to surrender his nephew. The position of the Quraysh strongly influenced the other Arab tribes to oppose the Muslims. The pagan chiefs sent an ultimatum to the clan of the Prophet, demanding that he should be declared an outlaw and delivered to them for execution. Every member, including the polytheists among them, rejected the demand. Thereupon the chiefs determined to boycott the extended family of Muhammad and any who supported them. The Prophet's uncle, Abu Lahab, left his kinsmen and participated in the boycott in support of the enemies of Islam.

Men, women and children were deprived of food and supplies for nearly three years and endured extreme hardship. They were reduced to eating the leaves of bushes

31

and suffered terrible misery. Many of them died, but no one would defect or betray the Prophet. For his part, the Prophet never ceased reciting the revelations from Allah and teaching the religion at every opportunity.[35] Finally, a group of non-Muslims from different tribes moved by humanitarian sentiment denounced the unjust and oppressive boycott. Concurrently, a document declaring the boycott, which had been hung on the *Ka'bah,* was devoured by white ants, leaving only the words "In Your name, O Allah." Thus the boycott was finally lifted, and many of those who had been in Abyssinia returned, only to face renewed persecution later on.

The Prophet's wife, Khadijah, and his protecting uncle and chief of the tribe, Abu Talib, passed away soon after the boycott ended. Their death was not only a great personal loss but signaled the beginning of another difficult period for the Prophet of Allah. Abu Lahab, the ardent enemy of Islam, now succeeded to leadership of the tribe.

The Messenger then decided to make a journey to the neighboring city of Ta'if for the purpose of inviting its people to Allah. There he met the chiefs and leaders, calling upon them to worship God alone, but the chiefs were rude and insolent. They incited gangs of youths to harass and throw stones at him and drive him out of the city. Exhausted and injured, his only fear was that Allah might be displeased because he had somehow failed in his duty. During his return, while disheartened and depressed, Gabriel appeared with an angel who offered to crush the unbelievers of Makkah between two mountains. But the Prophet replied, "Rather, I hope that Allah will bring forth from their loins those who will worship Him alone without associating anything with Him."[36]

---

[35]This is a historical refutation of the false claim that Muhammad was an advocate of nationalism who represented the hopes and aspirations of the Arabs at that time. It shows that bonds of faith and common objective are stronger than those of blood or nationality.

[36]Narrated by al-Bukhari and Muslim.

In order to encourage and show favor upon Prophet Muhammad after the severe trials he had endured, his Lord honored him through the miraculous night journey (*israa'*) to Jerusalem and ascension (*mi'raaj*). It is mentioned thus in the Qur'an: **"Exalted is He who took His servant by night from the Sacred Mosque [in Makkah] to the Farthest Mosque [in Jerusalem], whose surroundings We have blessed, to show him of Our signs."**[37]

From Jerusalem the Prophet was raised through the seven heavens during the same night. There he met several of the former prophets and was shown some of the greatest signs of God. It was there, as well, that Allah made five daily prayers obligatory. Details of the journey were related to the people the following morning. Muhammad was asked by the disbelievers to describe Jerusalem as proof to them, which he did accurately, additionally informing them of a caravan on its way to Makkah, which arrived at the predicted time. But in spite of that evidence, most of them refused to believe. The believers, however, had no doubt about this event, certain of the Prophet's truthfulness.

The Messenger of Allah continued to approach various tribes during their visits to Makkah and to the *Ka'bah*, asking them to acknowledge that God alone was worthy to be worshipped. He would say, "O people, declare that there is no god other than Allah, and you will attain success." But Abu Lahab would follow him, appearing wherever people assembled around him and shout, "He is misguided and a liar. He wants you to abandon your gods and goddesses. Do not let him lure you away from your religion and the religion of your forefathers." The Prophet would sometimes inquire of those present, "Would any man take me among his people since the Quraysh have prevented me from conveying the words of my Lord, the Mighty and Majestic?"[38]

---

[37]Qur'an, 17:1.
[38]Narrated by Ahmad.

Then, by the will of God, came the turning point for Islam. During the pilgrimage season some men from the northern city of Yathrib heard the Prophet speaking, accepted the truth of what he said, and swore allegiance to him. They returned with the message to their city, where more people entered the faith. Islam spread in Yathrib, and the following year a delegation was sent to invite the Messenger to their city and pledge that they would defend him as they would their own families.

The pagan establishment would never allow Muslims the freedom to practice their faith. Those who had endured unbearable conditions in Makkah were at last given permission to migrate to Yathrib. They moved quietly in order to avoid confrontation as much as possible, most being forced to abandon everything they owned. They left their homeland, their kinsmen and their properties, all for the cause of God, to uphold and spread the principles of His religion. But the Prophet himself remained behind, awaiting a divine command at the appropriate time, for the primary concern was to insure continuation of his mission.

The Quraysh, dismayed at the turn of events and the escape of so many Muslims from under their jurisdiction, convened once again, determined to end the challenge to their authority once and for all. About the same time that Allah directed His Messenger to emigrate from Makkah, the Quraysh were plotting his assassination. A member of each clan was to take part in the collaborated murder in order to avoid retribution by the heirs against any one of them. However, Allah inspired His Messenger with perception of the conspiracy, enabling him to elude his enemies and leave the city with his close companion, Abu Bakr.

It was only their stubbornness and attachment to influence and supremacy which prevented the unbelieving Quraysh from accepting Muhammad's message of reform. Strangely enough, they had entrusted some of their valuables to the care of the Prophet, evidence that they were well aware of his integrity. In fact, they had trusted him with their possessions even while they were opposing him and plotting his death. Before his departure from Makkah with his life in danger, the Messenger of Allah instructed that everything entrusted to his care by them be returned to the owners.

The Prophet's migration from Makkah to Yathrib is called the *Hijrah*.[39] All attempts of the Makkan polytheists to overtake him and prevent it ended in failure. There are authentic accounts of several incidents during the journey when the Prophet and his companion faced grave danger, but Allah protected them miraculously from harm.

Yathrib had been chosen by God to shelter His Messenger and to serve as a focal point for the universal call of Islam. Following the *Hijrah,* it came to be known as "*Madinat ar-Rasul*" (City of the Messenger), or simply, Madinah. Various cultures, religions and communities flourished in this city in contrast to Makkah, which was dominated by a single faith and cultural pattern.

The Madinan Period – Before Islam came to Madinah, its inhabitants belonged mainly to three communities: the two Arab tribes of Aus and Khazraj and the Jews, in whose hands was much of the city's wealth and who dominated its economy largely through the practice of monopoly and usury. Rifts between the two Arab tribes were promoted by the Jews who profited from money-lending toward war efforts and the sale of weapons. As a rule, the pagan inhabitants of Madinah followed the religious and social traditions of the Quraysh, as they were guardians of the *Ka'bah*.[40] Many of them also tended to respect the Jews and Christians for the books and the knowledge they possessed. And since their idol worship was fundamentally opposed to the message of monotheism, they viewed the

---

[39]This event was later designated as the beginning of the Islamic calendar.
[40]At that time, the *Ka'bah* representing monotheism, housed 360 idols in and around it.

attitude of the "People of the Scripture" as justification for refusal to accept the faith brought by Muhammad.

For their part, the Jews and Christians of the region were resentful of the Prophet because they felt that divine scripture should have been revealed to one of them rather than to an Arab, so the majority were openly hostile. Jealousy motivated them to join ranks with the pagans in opposition to Islam even after the fact of Muhammad's prophethood had become unmistakably clear.

For several centuries the Jews had been waiting for the prophet foretold in their scriptures. They often spoke of this expectation, and thus it was known to the Arabs, perhaps indirectly influencing the Aus and Khazraj tribes toward recognition of the Messenger once they heard about him. The number of Muslims from these two tribes had been steadily increasing. Upon receiving news of the Prophet's departure from Makkah, they eagerly awaited his arrival. The Muslims of Madinah welcomed him to their city with excitement and elation.

Believers continued to migrate from Makkah to Madinah until the only ones left were those who had been forcibly detained by the Quraysh. The Muslims of Madinah assisted the emigrants in a most generous manner, offering to share with them equally whatever they possessed, sometimes even depriving themselves to accommodate their brothers in faith. They were called *Ansaar* (Supporters), and the Prophet himself established a bond of brotherhood between them and the *Muhajireen* (Emigrants) in order to unite and strengthen the emerging Islamic society.

After thirteen years of oppression in Makkah, the faithful now had a community of their own. The first undertaking of the Prophet after arriving in Madinah was to begin construction of a permanent place of worship, a mosque. He then drew up peace agreements with the Jews of Madinah and Arab tribes of the surrounding

36

regions. With consent of the non-Muslim Arabs, the Jews, Christians and others, he established an Islamic state in which justice was guaranteed for all. Its written constitution – the first of its kind in world history – defined the rights and duties of both citizens and head of state and laid down principles of defense and foreign policy. It acknowledged that Prophet Muhammad would have the final word on any matter of disagreement while explicitly recognizing freedom of religion, particularly for the Jews, to whom the constitution afforded equality with Muslims in all that concerned life within the community.

Prior to the spread of Islam in Madinah and arrival of Allah's Messenger, the Aus and Khazraj as well as the Jews had agreed to recognize Abdullah bin Ubayy as their leader, and preparations were being made to crown him king. So when people began to desert him in favor of Islam, he perceived that the appearance of the Prophet in Madinah had deprived him of his kingship, and he was filled with rage and jealousy. Since most of the community were determined to embrace Islam, he went along with the tide and declared acceptance of it outwardly while retaining enmity in his heart. All those who had been ambitious for power and prestige were similarly outraged at the success of this new movement which had united the *Muhajireen* and *Ansaar* in allegiance to the Messenger of Allah. These formed a group of hypocrites who entered the religion deceptively and worked against it from within.

Not content with being rid of their Muslim citizens, the Quraysh in Makkah contacted Abdullah bin Ubayy. They sent him an ultimatum demanding that he hand over or at least expel the Prophet and his companions, otherwise they would launch a military offensive that would annihilate his army and take his women captive. Abdullah bin Ubayy responded positively to the Makkan polytheists and mobilized his supporters. On learning of this alliance, the Prophet advised Abdullah to be more rational and cautioned his men against being tricked into fighting against their own kinsmen. The men abandoned the idea so their chief had to comply, but he remained a dangerous ally of the angry Quraysh and envious Jews.

The revelation of Qur'anic verses to the Messenger of Allah continued regularly, providing constant guidance and direction for him and his followers. The style of revelation in Madinah was distinct from that of Makkan verses and dealt with different matters. Relationships with other peoples were defined, and the believers were repeatedly warned by Allah against both external enemies and internal weaknesses. The Qur'an exposed and warned against strategies of the hypocrites, their hidden agenda and concealed activities.

Divine legislation and instruction was eagerly awaited and immediately applied within the community of believers. The verses were being sent down in stages according to the needs and requirements of specific circumstances, giving certainty to the believers that Allah is aware of all things and that He was with them during every situation, no matter how difficult. At the same time, it contained the charter for an Islamic state as well as universal guidance for all mankind, applicable to every place and every age and valid until the end of time. The Qur'an is indeed the lasting miracle of God's final prophet.

Muslims who were unable to emigrate from Makkah had become the object of increasing vengeance of the Quraysh, but still no order to defend or retaliate had come from Allah. In desperation, the oppressed people called out to Him to save them from the ever-increasing persecution. At this precarious juncture, permission was finally given for the Muslims to fight because of the injustice done to them.

Provocations and skirmishes were to pave the way for a major confrontation between the Muslims and the polytheists. The Makkans threatened to exterminate the

Muslims in their new homeland of Madinah. When the Prophet received information from reliable sources attesting to the intrigues and plots being devised by the enemies of Islam, precautionary measures were taken and a state of alert was declared.

Then Allah revealed: **"Fight in the cause of Allah those who fight you, but do not commit aggression. Indeed, Allah does not like aggressors."**[41] Thus began the struggle to defend the infant state, to liberate mankind from the tyranny of other men, and to establish true worship of Allah upon the earth. This is an aspect of the term *"jihad."* But it is incorrect to assume that *jihad* is synonymous with war, for the word essentially means: a strenuous and sincere effort on the personal as well as the social level. It is a struggle to implement good and to remove injustice, oppression and evil from one's self and one's society. This effort is a spiritual, social, economic and political one.[42]

Trade caravans were essential to the continued prosperity of the Quraysh. Word reached Madinah that a caravan returning from Syria laden with goods would be passing within close range of the city. By intercepting the caravan the Muslims hoped to assert their influence and recover a small portion of what they had been forced to leave behind. However, since it was a commercial caravan, the Prophet did not make significant arrangements for fighting. Perceiving the possibility of a raid, the caravan's leader sent a call for help to the Quraysh, who immediately dispatched an army from Makkah. The result was the Battle of Badr. Upon seeing the Muslims

---

[41] Qur'an, 2:190.

[42] For example, one of the highest levels of *jihad* mentioned by the Prophet is to speak a word of truth to a tyrant. Restraining the self from wrongdoing is a form of *jihad*, and it also includes social reforms and efforts to eliminate ignorance, poverty, foreign domination, racial discrimination, religious persecution and oppression of every kind.

inadequately equipped and vastly outnumbered, the Prophet fervently supplicated his Lord for support. The small band of Muslims fought valiantly, and as Allah revealed in the Qur'an, He reinforced them with a thousand angels. The amazing victory at Badr established the Muslim community as a political entity and gained it prestige among the neighboring tribes.

One year later, burning with the desire for revenge, the Prophet's enemies amassed an army three times larger than before. Revelation came down from Allah ordering the believers to defend and strike back.[43] The Messenger of Allah decided it would be best to face them in his own territory, so the armies met at Mount Uhud. Again the Muslims, whose numbers were small in comparison, fought courageously. They were on the verge of victory when a faction of the army, using their own judgement and disobeying the Prophet's orders, caused a weakness in the ranks which was exploited by the enemy. This led to a setback for the Muslims, the loss of many lives, and the wounding of the Prophet – a costly mistake but a valuable lesson for the believers.

After the Battle of Badr, one of the Jewish tribal chiefs proceeded to Makkah to reconfirm his alliance

---

[43]Qur'anic verses concerning battle are often quoted out of their historical context to allege that Islam promotes violence and exhorts its followers to kill non-Muslims. However, these verses, without exception, address aggressions committed against Muslims during the time of the Prophet. *Jihad* in the form of armed struggle becomes an option only after the failure of all peaceful measures; and then, it can only be declared by the religious leadership or head of a Muslim state. Moreover, it is subject to strict regulations. The Messenger emphatically prohibited the killing of non-combatants, and the Qur'an instructs: **"And if they incline to peace, then incline to it [also] and rely upon Allah. Indeed, He is the Hearing, the Knowing."** (8:61) Islam forbids injustice, even toward those who oppose the religion. Enmity toward any people or nation should never provoke Muslims to commit aggression against them, oppress them or disregard their rights, as stated in the Qur'an (see 5:8).

40

with the pagans and incite them to a war of revenge. Following the Battle of Uhud, the same Jewish leader and his men conspired to assassinate the Prophet by dropping a large stone on him from the top of a wall, but Allah again protected His Messenger. In spite of their treachery, the only demand made of this tribe was that they leave the region of Madinah.

Two years later the Quraysh amassed an even larger force and made alliances with other pagan tribes and the exiled Jewish clans as well as the Jews who remained inside Madinah. They did not hesitate to violate their agreement with the Prophet since they expected his defeat at the hands of the powerful alliance. The coalition planned and mobilized for an invasion.

Upon obtaining this information, the Prophet and his companions prepared for defense of Madinah. They spent days and nights digging a trench around the vulnerable part of the city to keep the attacking armies at bay. The coalition of enemy forces besieged the city for three weeks. There were also enemies from within – the Jews who had defected and Arab hypocrites secretly working against the state. After a tense and difficult period in which their defense was nearly broken, the Muslims turned in fervent supplication to their Lord. Thereupon, Allah sent a violent wind against the enemy camp, wrecking havoc therein, terrifying them and forcing them to withdraw. This encounter, known as the Battle of al-Khandaq (or al-Ahzaab), was the last attempt by the Quraysh to destroy the Muslim base.

In the following period it was necessary to subdue the Jews who had violated their treaty with the state, as well as those polytheistic tribes which were a continuing threat. But during this time as well, many of the neighboring tribes, hearing of the "new" religion and sending emissaries to inquire about it, entered Islam. This active period also witnessed several of the Prophet's marriages, all of which were contracted for political and social reasons or out of

41

mercy for widows who had suffered for the cause of Islam.[44]

In the sixth year after the *Hijrah* the Prophet and a large company of his companions set out for Makkah with the intention of performing the rites of *'Umrah*.[45] Alarmed at growing Muslim influence, the Quraysh sought to prevent them, and met them a short distance from Makkah. After a session of difficult negotiations, they established a ten year agreement, called the Truce of Hudaybiyyah. Its conditions may be summarized as follows:

- Both parties would observe a state of peace and not interfere with the free movement of the other.
- Every tribe would be allowed to enter into an alliance with either party and become a participant in the treaty.
- The *'Umrah* would be postponed until the following year. At that time, the Muslims would be permitted to stay in Makkah for three days only.
- Any man leaving the Quraysh to join the Muslims must be sent back, but any man coming from the Muslims to Quraysh would not be sent back.

The Quraysh of Makkah were pleased with this treaty so seemingly to their advantage. Although they were reluctant to accept its terms and viewed it as a setback, the companions complied out of faith in their Prophet, who had agreed to the conditions. But Allah distinctly referred to it in the Qur'an as a "clear victory," and those who had first considered it a concession came to understand its benefit and wisdom thereafter. This truce was, in fact, a formal recognition of the Muslim state and

---

[44]After the death of Khadijah and before the *Hijrah*, the Prophet married Sawdah, a widow, and A'ishah, the daughter of his closest companion, Abu Bakr. The rest of his marriages took place after his residence in Madinah.

[45]The lesser pilgrimage to the *Ka'bah*, which may be done at any time of the year.

of the right of all people to practice and invite others to their religion.

The following year Makkah was temporarily evacuated by the Quraysh, and the Messenger with 2,000 of his followers were allowed to perform *'Umrah*. Observing them from the surrounding hills, the Makkans were impressed by the sight, and many conversions to Islam took place.

Even before the Treaty of Hudaybiyyah and despite his demanding responsibilities as head of state, the Prophet had been resolutely teaching the religion ordained by Allah. But it was as yet confined to the region of Madinah due to the belligerent activities of the Quraysh and their widespread influence. The ten-year truce provided a cessation of hostilities between the Quraysh and Muslims, during which the Prophet could freely send his representatives on missions to make the religion known throughout the Arabian peninsula. This he did with remarkable results.

Among the objections to Islam cited by pagan chiefs who rejected any concept of accountability for their actions was belief in the Hereafter and its balance of just compensation. They asserted that restoration of life after death is impossible, simply because no man had ever witnessed it. But the Qur'anic verses recited by the Prophet offered the logical answer that the present creation is in itself a clear sign of Allah's ability to create and re-create as He wills. **"Is not He who created the heavens and earth able to create the likes of them?"**[46] **"Do they not see that Allah, who created the heavens and earth and did not fail in their creation, is able to give life to the dead?"**[47] **"Does man not remember that We created him before, while he was nothing?"**[48] **"And you have already**

---

[46]Qur'an, 36:81.

[47]Qur'an, 46:33.

[48]Qur'an, 19:67. It is to be noted that God's reference to Himself as "We" in many Qur'anic verses is understood in the Arabic language to denote grandeur and power, not plurality.

known the first creation, so will you not be reminded?"[49]
Many found this reasoning compelling enough to dispel
all doubt. Other issues of faith were progressively being
resolved in the same way – through divine revelation to
the Messenger of Allah.

As he was commissioned by Allah to address all of
mankind, Prophet Muhammad campaigned intently for
the return to pure monotheism and to divinely ordained
moral values among the peoples of the world. Profiting
from the period of peace, he now launched an intensive
program for the propagation of Islam and extended his
message into lands beyond the frontiers of Arabia. He
sent emissaries who, in addition to their dedication and
extensive knowledge of the religion, were acquainted with
the culture and language of the peoples to whom they
were sent. The Prophet dispatched letters to rulers of
Byzantium, Persia, Abyssinia, Egypt, Damascus, Bahrain,
Yamamah, Oman and other provinces, some of whom
responded favorably, while others refused out of arrogance
or fear of losing power.

Because common people are likely to follow the
customs, ideologies and incentives of their leaders, the
Messenger of Allah addressed several letters to the most
influential rulers of neighboring nations and empires,
inviting them to Islam. Only a prophet of God sent on a
divine mission would dare to summon imperious autocrats
to accept his prophethood. Such a man could not harbor
the least doubt about the success of his sacred mission.
His conviction regarding the support and capability of his
Lord was such that the proudest sovereign did not appear
to him anything more than a puppet whose strings were
held in the hand of Allah. Whatever responses he received,
the Prophet and his message had now been acknowledged
by the major powers of the day.

---

[49]Qur'an, 56:62.

The universal nature of Islam was confirmed early in the Prophet's mission while a small number of his followers were being oppressed in Makkah. At that time Allah had revealed: **"And We have not sent you except as a mercy for the worlds."**[50] Again, while yet in Makkah, Allah instructed him: **"Say, 'O mankind, indeed I am the Messenger of Allah to you all, [from Him] to whom belongs the dominion of the heavens and the earth. There is no god except Him; He gives life and causes death. So believe in Allah and His Messenger, the unlettered prophet, who believes in Allah and His words, and follow him that you may be guided.'"**[51]

Of the communications sent to foreign heads of state by the Prophet, those to the Negus (King of Abyssinia), to Heraclius (Byzantine Emperor), to the Muqawqis (Ruler of the Copts in Egypt) and to Chosroes (Emperor of Persia) are the most well-known. Each of his letters began in the name of Allah, and their substance may be summarized as follows:

From Muhammad, Messenger of God, to the Negus, Grand Ruler of Abyssinia:

Peace be upon him who follows right guidance. I praise Allah (God), other than whom there is no deity, and I testify that Jesus, the son of Mary, is the Spirit of God, and His Word which He sent to Mary, the good and pure virgin. She conceived Jesus through His spirit and His breath just as He created Adam by His hand and His breath. I invite you to God, who is one without any associate, and to His obedience, and to follow me and believe in what has come to me, for I am the Messenger of God. I invite you and your men to God, the Mighty and Majestic. I have communicated this, so accept my advice.[52]

50Qur'an, 21:107. Again, "We" denotes the grandeur and power of Allah.
51Qur'an, 7:158.
52The Negus replied positively and embraced Islam.

From Muhammad, Messenger of God, to Heraclius, Emperor of Rome:

Peace be upon him who follows right guidance. I hereby invite you to Islam. Accept Islam; you will be in peace and God will give you your reward doubled. But if you do not, the sin of your subjects will [also] be upon you. **"O People of the Scripture, come to a word that is equitable between us and you – that we will not worship except Allah and not associate anything with Him and not take one another as lords instead of Allah."**[53]

From Muhammad, Messenger of God, to Chosroes, Emperor of Persia:

Peace be upon him who follows right guidance, believes in God and His Messenger, and testifies that there is no god but Allah alone with no associate and that Muhammad is His servant and messenger. I invite you to God, for I am the Messenger of God to all people, to warn those who are alive and verify [His] decree against the disbelievers. Accept Islam and you will be in peace. But if you refuse, the sin of the fire worshippers will [also] be upon you.[54]

* * *

Not even three years had passed following the Treaty of Hudaybiyyah when the Quraysh violated their

---

[53]The Qur'anic verse quoted is 3:64. The letter addressed to the Muqawqis in Egypt was worded similarly. Both Christian rulers acknowledged the truth of the message but worldly concerns prevented them from entering Islam.

[54]Upon receipt of the letter, Chosroes angrily tore it up and ill-treated the Prophet's envoy. The Prophet remarked that his empire would soon be torn up. This occurred within a period of eight years, as it fell bit by bit to the advancing Muslims and most of the population entered Islam.

obligations.[55] Their attempts to deceive the Prophet about the matter failed, and in the eighth year after the *Hijrah* a Muslim army of 10,000 led by the Prophet of Allah marched towards Makkah. Nearing the city, the Prophet's uncle, Abbas, encountered Abu Sufyan, then leader of the Quraysh, and advised him to join the Prophet and avert bloodshed. Abu Sufyan accompanied him to the Prophet's campsite and declared his acceptance of Islam. In a gesture of generosity the Prophet promised that anyone who entered the house of Abu Sufyan would be safe, as well as those who entered the Sacred Mosque in which was the *Ka'bah*. The leader of the Quraysh returned to Makkah, warning his people that resistance would be of no avail against the Muslim forces. So they apprehensively awaited the army's approach.

The army of companions had been divided into two factions, one led by the Prophet and one by his brilliant commander, Khalid bin al-Waleed. Khalid's faction was met by allies of the Quraysh who attempted to prevent them from entering the city but were easily overcome. The Prophet's faction met no resistance at all. In a manner so unlike that of an arrogant conqueror, Prophet Muhammad entered the city whose people had been a source of abuse and injury for twenty years, bowed humbly and gave thanks to Allah for His great favor and the victory for Islam.

The *Ka'bah,* built for Allah and the very symbol of monotheism, had been turned into a house of idols and images, housing 360 objects of worship in and around it. Upon entering Makkah, Prophet Muhammad proceeded to the House of Allah. He circled it seven times as prescribed, while breaking the idols in his path and

---

[55]Prophet Muhammad always adhered to the terms of treaties of which he was a party. He honored all promises and pacts and ordered his followers to do the same. Among the cardinal principles of his policy was that whenever he made an agreement, he abided by it strictly until it was violated by an enemy.

reciting: **"The truth has come and falsehood has perished. Indeed, falsehood [by nature] is bound to perish."**[56] The door of the *Ka'bah* was opened, and Allah's Messenger had the pictures within it effaced and all the idols destroyed, thereby purifying the House for the worship of Allah alone, as it was always meant to be. He then entered and prayed to his Lord inside the *Ka'bah*.

Then he came out, returned the key to its traditional custodian, and addressed the Quraysh, saying, "What do you suppose I should do with you?" In spite of their former animosity, they knew him. They replied, "What is good. You are a generous brother and the son of a generous brother." Said the Messenger of Allah, "No blame will there be on you today. Go, for you are free."

Thus did Almighty Allah open the hearts of the people to Islam. After observing that justice was truly established, the former enemies came to the Prophet, asking for forgiveness and declaring their commitment to Islam. And he accepted them all. Even those who had joined the Muslims initially for worldly advantage or material gain now accepted the religion from their hearts, dedicating themselves sincerely to Allah.

The Prophet remained in Makkah for nineteen days during which he gave numerous addresses, teaching the religion and explaining its legislation. He also sent deputies to destroy the temples of pagan gods in the areas surrounding the city and received delegations and individuals pledging allegiance to Allah and His Messenger. The liberation and complete transformation of Makkah was accomplished within these few days.

However, the neighboring city of Ta'if remained hostile and was determined to defend its idols. They also aspired to defeat the Muslims in order to replace the Quraysh as custodians of the *Ka'bah*. Their armies

---

[56]Qur'an, 17:81.

assembled and advanced toward Makkah. In order to avoid bloodshed in the vicinity of the *Ka'bah,* the Prophet led his forces out of the city to meet them. They were made up of the 10,000 who had accompanied him from Madinah joined by another 2,000 from the newly converted youths of Makkah. A bit overconfident due to their now greater numbers, the Muslims were at first somewhat careless in this encounter, leading to losses and the wounding of the Prophet. Yet, in the end they were victorious by the will of Allah. Again, no retribution was carried out against the people of Ta'if.

Fearing the expansion of the Prophet's influence and authority in Arabia, the oppressive Byzantine Empire amassed troops in preparation for an attack. In response to this the Prophet organized a march to the north. The long and difficult journey was yet another test for the believers, and upon finally reaching the settlement of Tabuk, they found the Romans had withdrawn. Not long after the Prophet's death, the mighty empires of Rome and Persia were defeated, liberating the peoples under their occupation who gladly sought refuge in the justice of Islam.

In the tenth year following the *Hijrah,* a great multitude of Muslims from Madinah joined by others from every part of the Arabian peninsula accompanied the Messenger of Allah to Makkah to perform the rites of *Hajj.*[57]

It was during this pilgrimage that Allah revealed verses which alluded to the fact that Prophet Muhammad's mission on earth was completed and that the time of his death was near. And it was then that he gave what is known as his "farewell address" in which he clarified and confirmed many aspects of the law and in which he called for justice to all people.

---

[57]The greater pilgrimage, required of every Muslim who is physically and financially able once in a lifetime.

He explained the fundamental principles of Islam and denounced polytheism and ignorance. He declared life, honor and property to be inviolable and that all practices of the pagan past were now abolished. He addressed the rights of women and servants. He requested those present to pass on what they had heard to those who were absent, finally inquiring of them, "Have I conveyed the message?" Upon hearing their unanimous reply to the affirmative, he concluded, "O Allah, witness it." After the pilgrimage the Prophet remained in Makkah for ten days and then returned to Madinah.

The greatest longing of Prophet Muhammad was to meet his Lord, and now Allah was to permit him to leave this transitory world of test and trial for the eternal home where his wish would be fulfilled. The Prophet had completed his work on earth and discharged his trust. Early in the eleventh year he became ill. Perceiving the end was near, he addressed the people, inquiring whether he had wronged anyone or owed something to anyone, not wishing to leave behind the least liability. He continued to offer advice and warnings and to lead the people in congregational prayer. Finally, pain and fever so weakened him that he ordered Abu Bakr to lead the prayer in his place. He passed away three days later.

The companions were profoundly grieved, not only by the loss of their beloved Prophet but also because they knew there would be no further revelation from Allah. But as Abu Bakr declared to those still in shock and disbelief at the news: "If any worshipped Muhammad – Muhammad is dead. But whoever worships Allah – Allah is the Ever-Living, who will never die." And he recited the verse: **"Muhammad is not but a messenger. Many messengers have passed on before him. So if he was to die or be killed, would you turn back on your heels [to disbelief]?"**[58]

---

[58]Qur'an, 3:144.

At the time of the Prophet's death, most inhabitants of the Arabian peninsula and the southern regions of Iraq and Palestine had voluntarily embraced Islam. Those Christians, Jews and Persians who remained attached to their own religions were granted freedom of belief as well as judicial, juridical and cultural autonomy. On numerous occasions he had upheld and emphasized the rights of non-Muslim citizens and had said, "Whoever harms a non-Muslim [within our state] will have me as his adversary, and I will be his adversary on the Day of Resurrection."[59]

Muhammad was sent as a mercy from God to all of mankind. To posterity he left a creed of pure monotheism, including comprehensive legislation based on a system of moral values. The teachings of God's final messenger live on through the authentic narrations found in volumes of *hadith* literature. Second only to the Qur'an, these narrations are held as proof in any cases of doubt or disagreement about what is allowed, prohibited or preferable within the religion, since the Prophet's authority is derived from the divine will.[60]

---

[59]Narrated by al-Bukhari.

[60]In addition to the verses commanding him to convey and explain His message, Allah stated about His Messenger: **"He does not speak of his own inclination. It is not but an inspiration revealed."** (53:3-4)

PART TWO

ASPECTS OF THE PROPHET'S SUNNAH

In his farewell address during the *Hajj,* the Messenger of Allah informed the large gathering of Muslims and all future generations that they would not fall into error so long as they adhered to the Book of Allah (the Qur'an) and *sunnah* of His Prophet. *"Sunnah"* in Islamic terminology means the divinely ordained way or method followed by Prophet Muhammad, and is derived from the body of *saheeh* (authentic) and *hasan* (acceptable) *hadith* literature. In turn, the Prophet's *sunnah* is followed by Muslims as the best means to obtain Allah's approval and His reward in the life to come.

The *sunnah* is known through study of the confirmed narrations and the explanation of their meanings and proper application by qualified and trustworthy Muslim scholars. The study of *hadiths* is aimed at correctly understanding the rulings and lessons they contain, for they deal with what is obligatory, permitted or prohibited and demonstrate correct methods of worship. They also reveal the core aspects of belief, mentality and behavior expected of human beings by their Creator. Unfortunately, much of the latter has been disregarded within Muslim populations of recent times. But the fact remains that all prophetic observations were spoken and recorded for the very reason that they are important elements of the religion, and as such cannot be ignored.

Several verses of the Qur'an order obedience to the Messenger as a manifestation of obedience to Allah. Muslim scholars all agree that obedience to the Prophet after his death is in adherence to his *sunnah.* The final Messenger was sent not only to pass on the message as Allah revealed it to him but to explain it and put it into practice as an appropriate pattern of conduct that is not beyond the capabilities of ordinary human beings.

Hadith narrations illustrate how he exemplified and elaborated on the principles laid down in the Qur'an, providing guidelines for their correct interpretation and application. For example, in the Qur'an, Allah orders prayer. But it is from the *sunnah* that one learns the times and conditions for prayer and how to perform it. In fact, everything in the *sunnah* was directly or indirectly addressed by Allah in the Qur'an. And the entire *sunnah* is included in the verse which orders: **"Whatever the Messenger has given you – take; and what he has forbidden you – desist."**[61]

The Prophet's *sunnah,* when taken in entirety, offers a balanced view of the Islamic faith, worship, education and discipline he advocated, one that compliments and completes the basic religious obligations that every Muslim is required to observe and obey. Beyond statements of legal rulings and merits of worship, his sayings reflect particular objectives of Islam.

In the following sections, statements of Prophet Muhammad are given in italics. All of them have been confirmed as authentic by scholars of *hadith,* and their narrators and degree of acceptability are cited in footnotes.[62] People can benefit greatly by reflecting upon these words, relating them to their own situations, and putting them into practice whenever possible. For the *sunnah* relates to contemporary human existence, and indeed remains valid for all time to come as the foundation for a higher plane of civilization.

In the Realm of Belief – In addition to the basic pillars of faith,[63] the Islamic creed of required beliefs includes everything stated as fact in the Qur'an and in

---

61 Qur'an, 59:7.

62 *Hadiths* narrated by al-Bukhari or by Muslim are almost always graded as *saheeh* (authentic).

63 Which are: belief in God, His angels, His books, His messengers, the Last Day and predestination.

53

the verified *hadiths* of Prophet Muhammad. The Messenger of Allah passed on some interesting and vital information about God and His creation, about the nature of His religion, and about experiences of man during his worldly life and the results he will find in the eternal life to come. Knowledge of these realities provides a healthy perspective of the world as well as a basis for dealing with an increasingly challenging and often stressful existence.

Prophet Muhammad was a human being, and as such, he had no knowledge outside of that granted to him by Allah. However, as a sign of his prophethood, he was provided with particular information through divine inspiration that others did not possess. Describing the beginning of creation, he said:

"There was Allah, and there was nothing other than Him. His Throne was over water, and He wrote everything in the register, and He created the heavens and the earth."[64] *"The first thing Allah created was the pen, and He said to it, 'Write.' It said, 'O Lord, what shall I write?' He said, 'Write the destiny – what has been and whatever will be forever.'"*[65] *"When Allah created the creation, He wrote in the register that is with Him above the Throne, 'My mercy overcomes My anger.'"*[66]

Divine mercy will be fully manifested for believers in the life to come. But even in this world it is often evident in subtle ways. While everyone can expect to suffer a certain degree of physical and mental distress during his lifetime on earth, a Muslim believer benefits from the misfortunes and hardships of worldly life whenever he endures them patiently, anticipating full compensation with additional bounty in the greater, eternal life. Allah's Messenger declared:

---

[64]Narrated by al-Bukhari.
[65]Narrated by at-Tirmidhi – *saheeh*.
[66]Narrated by al-Bukhari and Muslim.

"Paradise is surrounded by difficulties, and the Hellfire is surrounded by desires."[67] *"The world is a prison for the believer and a paradise for the unbeliever."[68]* *"No person has been provided with anything better or more comprehensive than patience."[69]*

For the believer, patience to endure difficulties and the temporary restrictions of this world, deferring immediate satisfaction for a greater aim, results in the attainment of complete gratification in the next life. He is aware that there is no benefit in anger or impatience, and that on the contrary, trials and afflictions are opportunities to earn unlimited rewards through forbearance and prudent behavior. The Prophet gave insight into such matters:

"No Muslim is afflicted by worry, distress, fatigue or illness, even the prick of a thorn, but that Allah will remove through it some of his sins."[70] *"A man is given trials according to his religion. If there is firmness in his religion, his trial is increased; but if there is weakness in his religion, then it is lightened. Tribulations remain with the servant until he walks upon the earth having no sin left upon him."[71]*

"Amazing is the affair of a believer; all of it is good, and that is for no one but the believer. When he is touched with benefit, he is grateful and that is best for him. And when he is touched by misfortune, he is patient and that is best for him."[72] *"Nothing afflicts a believer of weariness, grief, prolonged suffering or even a concern that worries him but that Allah removes thereby some of his misdeeds."[73]*

---

[67]Narrated by Ahmad and Muslim.

[68]Narrated by Ahmad and Muslim. Believers restrict themselves from unlawful pleasures during the worldly life out of fear and love of Allah. While criminals and sinners might enjoy their present temporary existence to the full, in the next life they will pay the price of transgressions.

[69]Narrated by al-Hakim – *saheeh*.

[70]Narrated by al-Bukhari.

[71]Narrated by at-Tirmidhi – *hasan-saheeh*.

[72]Narrated by Muslim.

[73]Narrated by at-Tirmidhi – *saheeh*.

The Messenger informed people of another important aspect of divine mercy. Because Allah is entirely familiar with each of His servants and completely aware of their aims and intentions, they will never be misunderstood by their Lord at the time of Judgement and therefore can expect from Him absolute and perfect justice.

"Allah, the Exalted, has overlooked for my people the error [they committed], what was forgotten [by them], and what they were compelled to do."[74]

The reference here is specifically to that which is done or neglected unintentionally, because obviously, deliberate premeditated transgressions are never overlooked by Allah. Justice demands that they be subject to account on the Day of Judgement unless the wrongdoer repents from the sin sincerely before his death.

The Prophet often reminded man of his Creator's perfect awareness of his every deed, word, thought and intent. Through such knowledge one can avoid inappropriate thoughts and actions and can mentally interact with his Lord in a positive way throughout his life.

"Allah does not look at your bodies or faces, but He looks at your hearts and deeds."[75] *"Get to know Allah in times of ease, and He will know you in times of difficulty."*[76]

"Whoever would like to meet Allah – Allah will like to meet him. And whoever would not like to meet Allah – Allah will not like to meet him."[77] *"Allah, the Exalted, has said, 'I am with My servant when he thinks of Me; so let him think of Me whatever he will.'"*[78]

---

[74]Narrated by Ahmad – *saheeh*. This assumes that the overall mindset of believers is one of righteousness, so that what is done without their conscious intent is overlooked.

[75]Narrated by Muslim.

[76]i.e., His help will be near. Narrated by Ahmad – *saheeh*.

[77]Narrated by al-Bukhari and Muslim.

[78]Narrated by Ahmad, at-Tabarani and al-Hakim – *saheeh*.

The non-believer thinks negatively of his Lord, assuming that He does not exist or that He created man unjustly for no purpose. Hence, he has no desire to meet Him. And at the time of death he will dislike that meeting intensely and fear it, for then he will have become fully aware that all he had previously denied is an inescapable reality. In contrast, the righteous believer cannot but think most highly of Allah. He is eager to meet Him and to experience His justice, mercy and approval. Another narration gives him encouragement and reassurance:

"Allah, the Exalted has said, 'I am with my [righteous] servant when he thinks of Me, and I am with him when he remembers Me. So if he remembers Me to himself, I remember him to Myself; and if he remembers Me in a company, I remember him in a company better than them. If he approaches Me a hand span, I approach him an arm's length. And if he approaches Me an arm's length, I approach him the expanse of open arms. If he comes to Me walking, I come to him running.'"[79]

The Prophet added, *"The comparison of one who remembers Allah and one who does not is like that of the living and the dead."*[80] And he himself used to supplicate, *"O Allah, help me to remember You, to be grateful to You, and to worship You well."*[81]

He also encouraged study, contemplation and reflection upon life and the occurrences which affect individuals, communities and nations.

"For everything there is a reality, and a servant does not attain the reality of faith until he knows that whatever struck him could not have missed him and whatever

---

[79]Obviously, since the Creator bears no resemblance to His creation, the meaning is not to be taken in a physical sense. Narrated by al-Bukhari and Muslim.

[80]Narrated by al-Bukhari.

[81]Narrated by Ahmad – *saheeh*.

missed him could not have struck him."[82]   "For whomever Allah wishes good, He gives him understanding of the religion."[83]

The Messenger was aware that Allah, the Mighty and Majestic, has subjected His creation to certain natural laws. There are physical laws governing the operation of the entire universe from the huge galaxies to the tiniest atoms. There are laws governing life and death. And there laws governing occurrences in the present existence and others created for the Hereafter.

The present universe and everything that happens within it is due to the Creator's law of cause and effect. It began when Allah, the primary cause of all things, willed to bring it into existence, and thus it was created. And when He willed to give man the freedom to choose and follow his own course in life, He informed him that naturally, according to this same law, there would be consequences for his actions in both this life and the next. And He warned in the Qur'an:

"Whatever strikes you of disaster – it is for what your hands have earned; and He pardons much."[84]   "And beware of a trial that will not strike those who have wronged among you exclusively, and know that Allah is severe in penalty."[85]

The Messenger explained:

"When Allah sends down punishment on a people, it afflicts whoever is among them; but then they will be resurrected [individually] according to their deeds."[86]

Thus, during the period of worldly existence, the condition of any people or nation is determined by its

---

82Narrated by Ahmad – *saheeh.*
83Narrated by al-Bukhari and Muslim.
84Qur'an, 42:30.
85Qur'an, 8:25.
86Narrated by Ahmad and al-Bukhari.

majority. The Muslim nation is no exception. Whenever most Muslims were conscious of Allah, obedient to Him, honest and productive, their society reflected these values, and consequently justice and prosperity prevailed. The few who deviated and departed from the right path did not have a noticeable effect on community wellbeing. On the other hand, when great numbers of people forgot Allah, became self-serving, irresponsible and corrupt, Allah allowed their societies to decline accordingly. The righteous but weak minority could neither prevent the outcome nor escape its overall effect.

In the Hereafter, however, the results of good and evil are manifested for every person individually, as stated in the *hadith.* Each one will be precisely judged and justly compensated according to Allah's perfect knowledge of his general attitude and unique situation during his period of existence on the earth.

Thus, Islam is not based on magic formulas or wishful thinking. Benefit and advantage are accomplished through planning and persistent effort, while neglect allows dissolution and decline. This is true for everyone, believers and non-believers alike. The Prophet disclosed:

"Allah does not punish ordinary people for the deeds of leaders until the leaders do that which the people are able to correct but they do not correct it. That is when Allah will permit the destruction of both the people and the leaders."[87] *"When people see wrongdoing and do not correct it or see an oppressor and do not prevent him, Allah will be ready to include them all in His penalty."*[88]

Nonetheless, he supplicated to his Lord for the just remuneration of rulers, administrators and others in responsible positions according to their conduct: *"O Allah, whoever has been given authority over my people and makes difficulty for them, then make difficulty for him; and*

---

[87]Narrated by at-Tabarani.
[88]Narrated by Ahmad, Abu Dawud and at-Tirmidhi – *saheeh.*

whoever has been given authority over my people and is considerate of them, then be considerate of him."[89] This is general for all time to come, and the Messenger's supplications have never gone unanswered.

Allah, the Exalted, revealed to Prophet Muhammad that He has given man a position of responsibility upon the earth, to improve and develop it, and to enhance the quality of human life. The early Muslims trained and educated by the Messenger were fully conscious that there is a cause for every occurrence; therefore, they utilized the natural laws established by Allah to achieve success. They dedicated themselves to the cause of Allah and employed only lawful methods to build their society and accomplish their objectives. They planned ahead, prepared well, anticipated dangers, practiced caution, applied statistics and strategies, and made maximum use of their minds and of available material means. Then they trusted and relied upon Allah, never forgetting that the result of every affair is in His hands and achieved by His permission.

Prophet Muhammad was much concerned with the welfare of all people, yet he had to inform them that Allah guides only those who are willing to be guided:

"The example of that with which Allah has sent me of guidance and knowledge is like a rain that falls on the ground, part of which is good, absorbing the water and producing much pasture and grassland. And within it [i.e., this area] are basins retaining water whereby Allah gives benefit to the people – they drink from them and irrigate and cultivate. Yet, it falls also on another [area] which is but barren valleys that do not retain water nor do they produce pasture. This is the example of one who is knowledgeable in the religion of Allah and benefits from that with which Allah has sent me, so he learns and teaches; and of one who pays no attention to it and does

---

89Narrated by Ahmad – *saheeh.*

not accept the guidance of Allah with which I have been sent."[90]

Even for the believer, adherence to the straight path is not always easy. Throughout the worldly life, people commonly have to struggle with negative thoughts and suggestions. But Allah's Messenger directed his followers how to deal with such matters:

"Strive for that which benefits you, seek help from Allah, and do not give up. If something should afflict you, do not say, 'If only I had done that, [the result] would have been such and such.' But say, 'What Allah decreed and willed He has done,' for 'if' opens the way for Satan."[91]

"Allah, the Exalted, has overlooked for my people that which occurs to one's mind as long as he does not speak of it or act upon it."[92]

"A faction of my community shall remain clearly [standing] on the truth. They will not be harmed by those who forsake them until the decree of Allah comes."[93]

"Remember often the destroyer of pleasures – death. For no one will remember it during a difficult time but that it will make it easier for him, and no one will remember it during a good time but that it will narrow it for him."[94]

And the Messenger of Allah cautioned that although the Hereafter is often seen by people as very distant in time, place or possibility, it is in reality as near as one's own departure from the present existence, beginning with his death, and that moreover, his final destination is being determined right now by that which he believes, intends and does in the present life.

---

[90]Narrated by al-Bukhari and Muslim.

[91]Narrated by Muslim.

[92]Narrated by al-Bukhari and Muslim.

[93]Narrated by Muslim.

[94]Narrated by al-Bayhaqi – *hasan*.

"Paradise is nearer to one of you than the strap of his shoe, and so is the Hellfire."[95] *"Allah, the Exalted, has said, 'By My might and My majesty, I will not combine for My servant two securities nor two fears. If he feels secure from Me in this world, I will make him fearful on the Day I gather My servants; and if he fears Me in this world, I will make him secure on the Day I gather My servants.'"*[96]

"When someone dies, he is shown his destination by morning and evening. If he is among the people of Paradise, then [he will see himself] among the people of Paradise; and if he is among the people of Hell, then [he will see himself] among the people of Hell."[97] *"A person will be [in the Hereafter] with those he loves."*[98]

The last statement, which was a cause for rejoicing among the Prophet's companions, assures those who love Allah, His Messenger and righteous believers of enjoying their company in Paradise. But it also holds a warning to those who prefer sinful, malicious or unworthy associates that they will join them in the Hellfire. Hence, one should consider carefully whom he chooses to love.

Among the basic tenets of Islam is individual accountability with knowledge that Allah is aware of all things. The natural consequence of one's intent and behavior, both positive and negative, is none but full compensation in the life to come. Restoration of the balance of justice in a more advanced stage of creation completes the story of human existence and is but another manifestation of the Creator's perfect scheme. In the next existence, new kinds of laws will be in operation. Among them is that punishment is in precise proportion to sin, while reward is multiplied many times over. And among them is that in contrast to the temporary nature

---

[95]Narrated by al-Bukhari.

[96]Narrated by al-Bazzar – *hasan*.

[97]Narrated by al-Bukhari.

[98]Narrated by al-Bukhari and Muslim.

of this world, the afterlife is eternal. It is the genuine existence which will prove the present life to be essentially insignificant, except for its being a period of trial and examination.

Knowledge of such matters contributes greatly to a person's success during the tests and trials of this world. It also keeps him in a healthy balance between fear and hope, both of which constantly motivate him toward seeking his Lord's forgiveness and approval. It was for this very purpose that the Prophet described some realities of the life to come:

"Allah, the Exalted said, 'I have prepared for My righteous servant [in the Hereafter] what no eye has seen, no ear has heard, and has never occurred to a human heart.'"[99]

*"Allah, the Exalted, extends the time of an oppressor; but when He seizes him, He will not let him escape. **And thus is the seizure of your Lord when He seizes the cities while they are transgressing. Verily, His seizure is painful and severe.**"*[100] *"Allah will grip the earth on the Day of Resurrection and fold up the heavens in His right hand. Then He will say, 'I am the Sovereign. Where are the kings of the earth?'"*[101]

"No one will enter Paradise except that he will be shown his place in the Hellfire if he had done evil – to increase his gratitude. And no one will enter the Hellfire except that he will be shown his place in Paradise if he had done good – to increase his regret."[102]

Regarding Manners and Character – After the initial Muslim victories that liberated people from the tyranny of tribal warlords and the oppression of Roman and Persian

---

[99]Narrated by al-Bukhari and Muslim.
[100]Narrated by Muslim. The Qur'anic reference is 11:102.
[101]Narrated by al-Bukhari and Muslim.
[102]Narrated by al-Bukhari.

occupation, Islam rapidly spread eastward to China, westward to Spain, and deep into Africa. This phenomenon was not due to further military conquest but to the exemplary personalities of energetic Muslims who traveled to their lands as tradesmen, workers and educators. In those early centuries of Islam, the Prophet's *sunnah* was the unmistakable model of conduct which formed a Muslim's character. Often, mere contact with Muslim believers was enough to interest the local population in the remarkable religion that had produced such a high standard of justice and morality among ordinary men.

Allah granted those Muslims success as a consequence of adherence to the *sunnah* in their public and private lives. This they did out of certain knowledge that it is the true means to their Lord's approval. On numerous occasions Allah's Messenger had affirmed, *"The most beloved of His servants to Allah is the best of them in character."*[103] *"There is nothing heavier on the balance than good character."*[104]

A person's character, unlike his physical appearance, is something that can be altered, and this is among the main purposes for which religion was ordained. Allah's Messenger provided warnings, encouragement and practical advice for the improvement of manners, behavior and character.

One positive aspect of a believer's character is satisfaction with whatever Allah has provided and decreed, appreciation of his Lord's blessings, and not being overly concerned with worldly pleasures and comforts. He can then turn more of his attention to things that will benefit him in the eternal life to come. The Prophet stated:

"Wealth is not in an abundance of goods, but it is in contentment of the soul."[105] *"Eat, drink, give charity and*

---

[103]Narrated by at-Tabarani – *saheeh*.
[104]Narrated by Ahmad – *saheeh*.
[105]Narrated by al-Bukhari and Muslim.

dress without extravagance or pride."[106] "What is little and sufficient is better than what is much and distracting."[107] "Look to him [whose condition is] below you and do not look to him above you, for that is more likely that you will not underestimate Allah's favor upon you."[108]

"Gabriel came to me and said, 'O Muhammad, live as long as you will, for indeed you will die. And love whom you will, but you will be leaving him. And do what you will, for you will be compensated for it. And know that the honor of a believer is his standing in night prayer and that his power is in freedom from dependency upon people.'"[109]

A man came to the Prophet and said, "O Messenger of Allah, direct me to a deed which, when I have done it, Allah will love me and people will love me." He replied, "Be indifferent toward [pleasures of] the world and Allah will love you, and be indifferent to what is in the hands of people and people will love you."[110]

The measure of Allah's love and honor for His righteous servant of good character may be shown in unexpected ways, but it is not always apparent from his condition in the present life. Allah's Messenger explained: "Within my people are those who, if one of them asked Allah for Paradise, He would grant it to him; but if he asked Allah for something from this world, He would not give it to him out of regard for him."[111]

Acquiring new qualities that build good character is possible with effort and discipline. The Prophet himself used to ask Allah to direct him to the best of manners and morals and enable him to practice them. He would say,

---

[106]Narrated by Ahmad – *saheeh.*

[107]Narrated by Abu Ya'laa – *saheeh.*

[108]Narrated by al-Bukhari.

[109]Narrated by al-Hakim – *hasan.*

[110]Narrated by Ibn Majah, at-Tabarani and al-Hakim – *saheeh.*

[111]i.e., in order to protect him from that which has no real benefit or might be harmful. Narrated by at-Tabarani – *hasan.*

"O Allah, guide me to the best manners; none can guide to the best of them but You. And turn away from me bad manners; none can turn them away from me but You."[112]

The Messenger of Allah had much to offer in the way of guidance in this respect. His general advice to those who inquired was, *"Say, 'I believe in Allah,' and then be upright."*[113] This concise answer shows that faith alone, or the claim of faith, is insufficient, and that words must be proven by deeds. A Muslim is required to be upright in all his dealings, and especially toward his Creator through careful obedience and sincere worship. Then, he must be honest, ethical and considerate with respect to all people, creatures and creations.

"Whoever would like to be saved from the Fire and enter Paradise should meet death believing in Allah and the Last Day, and should do to people as he would like done to him."[114] *"None of you [truly] believes until he likes for his brother what he likes for himself."*[115] *"Do not consider anything good as insignificant, even meeting your brother with a pleasant face."*[116] *"Allah is generous and loves generosity; and He loves high morality and hates base morality."*[117] *"The signs of a hypocrite are three: when he speaks, he lies; when he promises, he breaks it; and when he is entrusted, he betrays."*[118]

In addition to the Prophet's own words, there are *hadiths* in which his character was described by those who knew him. For example, a boy who served him for nine years said, "He was the best of people, the most generous of people, and the most courageous of people.

---

[112]Narrated by Muslim.
[113]Narrated by Muslim.
[114]Narrated by Muslim.
[115]Narrated by al-Bukhari and Muslim.
[116]Narrated by Ahmad and Muslim.
[117]Narrated by at-Tabarani and al-Hakim – *saheeh*.
[118]Narrated by al-Bukhari and Muslim.

He never said about anything I did, 'Why did you do that?' and he never mentioned my faults. He never even said, 'uff' to me."[119] His wife, A'ishah, replied to a man who inquired, "His manner was the Qur'an,"[120] meaning that he lived according to its teachings. She also said, "The Messenger of Allah never struck anyone with his hand, not a woman nor a servant, except when fighting for the cause of Allah. And he never took revenge on anyone who had harmed him, except that when a prohibition of Allah was violated, he would retaliate on behalf of Allah."[121] And he said, *"Allah has revealed to me that you should be modest so that no one shows conceit over another and no one tyrannizes another."*[122]

Consideration for others was noticeable in his day-to-day behavior. When leading the people in prayer, he would be brief so as not to cause them hardship; although while alone, he would prolong his prayer for lengthy periods, especially at night. When he heard something objectionable about someone, he would not mention his name in public but only say, *"What is the matter with people who do such and such?"*[123] He expressed anxiety for his followers and for the future of the Muslims, warning them to be alert and not to fall into practices that lead to individual failure or to collective decline and downfall: *"I do not fear for you from poverty, but I fear for you from competition in worldly increase. And I do not fear for you from error, but I fear for you from deliberate intent."*[124] Concern for all people was evident in the way he grieved for those who refused his message of truth and justice, preferring instead the path leading to Hellfire and eternal regret.

119Narrated by Muslim. "Uff" is an expression showing displeasure.
120Narrated by Ahmad and Muslim.
121Narrated by Muslim.
122Narrated by Muslim.
123Narrated by Abu Dawud – *saheeh*.
124Narrated by Ahmad and al-Hakim – *saheeh*.

A person of good character has been described as one who is not resentful, stingy or covetous, does not annoy people, and avoids insulting and backbiting. He is modest, dignified, truthful, patient and friendly. He is concerned with people but not intrusive; he strives to satisfy others; he is pleasant, appreciative, and sympathetic but not naive. He is committed, dedicated and alert, and he can be firm when necessary. This was the disposition of Allah's Messenger, whose awareness of real life situations prompted him to warn, *"The believer is not bitten from the same hole twice."*[125] And he advised, *"Love the one you love moderately, for perhaps he will be hated by you one day. And hate the one you hate moderately, for perhaps he will be loved by you one day."*[126] In addition, he pointed Muslims in the right direction by saying, *"Whoever loves for Allah and hates for Allah and gives for Allah and withholds for Allah has completed the faith."*[127]

The Prophet of Allah directed people how to recognize within themselves the signs of righteousness and wrongdoing, saying, *"Righteousness is good morals, and wrongdoing is that which wavers within yourself and you would dislike people to discover."*[128]

He taught through his own example, but his instructions and advice give additional emphasis.

"Let there be no harm [to anyone] and no harming [in reciprocation]."[129] *"Whoever of you sees a wrong – let him change it by his hand; and if he is not able, then with his tongue; and if he is not able, then with his heart, and that is the weakest of faith."*[130]

---

[125]Narrated by al-Bukhari.

[126]Narrated by at-Tirmidhi– *saheeh*.

[127]Narrated by Abu Dawud – *hasan*.

[128]Narrated by Muslim.

[129]Narrated by Ibn Majah and ad-Daraqutni – *hasan*.

[130]Narrated by Muslim. Thus, there is no faith in the heart of someone who does not dislike wrongdoing or find it objectionable.

"The believer who mixes with the people and is patient with their abuse is better than the believer who does not mix with the people and is not patient with their abuse."[131]

"Should I not inform you of the best witness? It is the one who produces his evidence before he is asked for it."[132] *"Make things easy and do not make them difficult; give good tidings and do not drive [people] away."*[133]

"May Allah have mercy on a man who is lenient when he sells, lenient when he buys, and lenient when he requests payment."[134] *"Those who are merciful will be given mercy by the Most Merciful. Have mercy upon those on the earth and you will obtain mercy from Him in the heaven."*[135]

"Do not envy one another; do not deceive one another; do not hate one another; do not turn your backs on one another; and do not intrude on the transactions of one another, but be, O servants of Allah, brothers."[136]

"From the excellence of a person's Islam is his leaving alone what does not concern him."[137] *"He is in a good state who is occupied with his own faults rather than the faults of [other] people."*[138]

"He who believes in Allah and the Last Day should say what is good or keep quiet."[139] *"Sufficient it is as a lie for a person to speak of everything he hears."*[140] *"Do not backbite Muslims or pursue their faults. For he who pursues the fault of his brother Muslim – Allah will pursue his fault;*

131Narrated by Ahmad and at-Tirmidhi – *saheeh*.
132Narrated by Muslim.
133Narrated by al-Bukhari.
134Narrated by al-Bukhari.
135Narrated by Ahmad, Abu Dawud and at-Tirmidhi – *saheeh*.
136Narrated by Muslim.
137Narrated by at-Tirmidhi – *hasan-saheeh*.
138Narrated by al-Bazzar – *hasan*.
139Narrated by al-Bukhari.
140Narrated by Muslim.

and when Allah pursues his fault, He will expose him, even if he should be in the interior of his house."[141]

"If someone insults you and describes you with a fault you do not have, do not describe him with a fault he does have. Rather, let him earn the sin, and you will have the reward; and do not curse anyone."[142]

The Messenger of Allah advocated tolerance, forgiveness and avoiding revenge. He said, *"Indeed, Allah is kind and loves kindness. He grants for kindness what He does not grant for harshness.*"[143] *"No household is given lenience but that it benefits them.*"[144] *"Allah does not increase His servant who pardons [others] except in honor.*"[145] He would excuse those who were offensive in their dealings with him on a personal level, but if the transgression had to do with disobedience to Allah or injustice to others, he would show his disapproval and anger and would not hesitate to take appropriate action. This is reflected in severe warnings to unrepentant transgressors:

"The most ruthless in punishing people in this world will be the most ruthlessly punished of people by Allah on the Day of Resurrection."[146] *"The most severely punished of people on the Day of Resurrection is an unjust leader.*"[147]

"Fear the supplication of one who is wronged, even a non-believer, for there is nothing to screen it [from Allah]."[148] *"For every traitor there will be a banner by which he will be known on the Day of Resurrection.*"[149]

---

[141]Narrated by Ahmad and Abu Dawud – *saheeh*.
[142]Narrated by Ibn Hibban – *saheeh*.
[143]Narrated by Muslim and Abu Dawud.
[144]Narrated by at-Tabarani – *saheeh*.
[145]Narrated by Muslim.
[146]Narrated by Ahmad – *saheeh*.
[147]Narrated by at-Tabarani – *hasan*.
[148]Narrated by Ahmad – *saheeh*.
[149]Narrated by al-Bukhari and Muslim.

"Among that which people knew from the words of former prophecy is, 'When you feel no shame, then do whatever you wish.'"[150] *"The worst of people is one that others leave alone out of fear of his evil."*[151]

The warnings issued by Allah's Messenger about punishments in the next life are balanced with countless indications of how to avoid them and attain Paradise through correct worship and righteous deeds. Study and reflection reveal that the Prophet's guidance is comprehensive, balanced and complete. He used a variety of approaches in dealing with different issues because conditions and personalities are diverse. He observed, *"Indeed, the religion is easy, and no one will make religion difficult but that it will overpower him. So do what is right, strive for perfection, receive good tidings [of reward], and seek help through prayer in the mornings, afternoons and some part of the night."*[152]

Regarding Deeds and Worship – Allah stated in the Qur'an that to worship Him is the purpose of human existence[153] and He stated that He gave man life on earth in order to test him as to who is best in deeds,[154] meaning the deeds one does while intending worship of Him. For any deed that is done or avoided while seeking the acceptance of Allah automatically becomes an act of worship. However, the Prophet affirmed that Allah does not benefit from the worship of His creations, nor does their refusal harm Him in the least. In reality, it is His servants who benefit from their worship and obedience, both in this life and the next, and this is another aspect of the Creator's unlimited mercy. Every effort in His path brings a beneficial result. To cite but a few examples of

---

150Narrated by al-Bukhari.
151Narrated by al-Bukhari.
152Narrated by al-Bukhari.
153See verse 51:56.
154See 18:7 and 67:2.

cause and effect given by the Prophet on the subject of worship:

"No people sit mentioning Allah except that the angels surround them, mercy covers them, tranquility descends upon them, and Allah mentions them to those near Him."[155]

"Recite the Qur'an, for it will come on the Day of Resurrection as an intercessor for those who recited it."[156] "Whoever is skillful in recitation of the Qur'an will be with the noble messenger angels, and whoever recites the Qur'an faltering while it is difficult for him will have two rewards."[157]

"The five [obligatory] prayers, Friday [prayer] to the next Friday, and Ramadhan [fasting] to the next Ramadhan are expiation for what occurred between them when the major sins are avoided."[158] "Extract the poor-due from your wealth, for it will purify you."[159] "For the fasting person at the time of breaking his fast is a supplication that is not refused."[160] "From one 'Umrah to the next is expiation [for sins], and the reward of a sinless Hajj is none but Paradise."[161]

"The best prayer after the obligatory one is prayer during the night."[162] "Our Lord, blessed and exalted is He, descends to the nearest heaven when the last third of the night remains and He says, 'Who will supplicate to Me so I will answer him? Who will ask Me so I will give him? Who will seek My forgiveness so I will forgive him?'"[163]

155Narrated by Muslim.

156Narrated by Ahmad and Muslim.

157Narrated by al-Bukhari and Muslim.

158Narrated by Muslim. Major sins are removed only through sincere repentance.

159Narrated by Ahmad – *hasan*.

160Narrated by Ibn Majah.

161Narrated by al-Bukhari and Muslim.

162Narrated by Muslim.

163Narrated by al-Bukhari and Muslim. Allah's descent is not a physical one like that of His creation; rather it indicates extra attentiveness.

Each of the preceding narrations illustrates that acts of worship motivated by conscientious obedience are causes of beneficial results. Prophet Muhammad mentioned this relationship between the cause and its effect as an encouragement for believers to make good use of the time, abilities, means and opportunities they possess for obtaining something desirable or advantageous.

Other *hadiths* disclose that the best and most beloved deeds to Allah are the religious obligations which He has ordained, so they must always be given priority by a believer. It is fulfillment of these obligations that earns the greatest benefits, and none of them can ever be replaced by voluntary worship of any kind. When a Muslim carries out his religious obligations, carefully observing their requirements and conditions, he has cleared himself of the sin of negligence and earned the generous reward due to him from Allah.

After completing his obligatory acts of worship, one may go on to obtain further benefit and become even closer to Allah. The Prophet reported that Allah, the Mighty and Majestic, said, *"My servant does not draw near to Me with anything more loved by Me than what [duties] I have imposed on him. And My servant continues to draw near to Me with additional works until I love him; and when I love him, I am his hearing with which he hears, his sight with which he sees, his hand with which he strikes, and his foot with which he walks. If he asks [something] of Me, I will surely give it to him; and if he seeks refuge with Me, I will surely grant it to him."*[164]

But worship is not limited to the formal rites of prayer, fasting, pilgrimage and the like. It includes everything that is pleasing to Allah of words, deeds, attitudes and intentions. And it includes compliance in the upright

---

[164]Narrated by al-Bukhari. Allah does not "become" part of His creation in the physical sense. Rather, the servant's perception and actions are guided by what Allah has ordained.

conduct ordered by Allah: honesty, opposing injustice, respect and good treatment of people, teaching knowledge, counseling, preventing harm and giving benefit; all these become forms of worship as long as they are intended by a believer for his Creator's acceptance. Many of the Prophet's *hadiths* demonstrate that the concept of worship is extensive and comprehensive. For example, he said:

"One who strives for [assistance of] the widow and the needy is like a fighter for the cause of Allah or like someone who prays by night and fasts by day."[165]

"Every good deed is a charity, and the one who directs to good is like one who does it."[166] *"There is no Muslim who plants a sprout or a seed from which a person, animal or bird will eat but that it will be counted for him as a charity."*[167] *"Among the best of deeds is making a believer happy; paying for him a debt; satisfying for him a need; relieving him of a problem."*[168]

Thus, it may be understood that nearness to Allah is attained primarily by behavior which is pleasing to Him. The methods to be employed toward this end have been outlined in the Qur'an and elaborated upon in greater detail within the *sunnah*. But the Prophet pointed out that the righteous act alone is insufficient. It must be accompanied by the correct intention, meaning that it is done solely for the acceptance of Allah and no one else, and for no other reason. That is how one's deeds become acts of worship and are distinguished from those of habit, custom or hypocrisy. The Prophet cautioned: *"Deeds are only by intentions, and every man shall have only what he intended."*[169] Thus, if he intended something

---

165Narrated by al-Bukhari and Muslim.

166Narrated by al-Bayhaqi – *saheeh*.

167That is, he will earn the reward of a charity every time any creature eats from it. Narrated by al-Bukhari and Muslim.

168Narrated by al-Bayhaqi – *saheeh*.

169Narrated by al-Bukhari and Muslim.

for the approval of his Creator, he will have that approval and its reward; and if he intended it for a worldly purpose, such as praise and recognition, he will have in this life what he sought but without Allah's approval and reward, for His justice is precise and perfect.

This aspect of the *sunnah* encompasses everything in a believer's life. In the Qur'an, Allah instructed His Messenger: **"And say, 'Work, for Allah will see your deeds, and [so will] His Messenger and the believers. And you will be returned to the Knower of what is concealed and what is witnessed, and He will inform you of what you used to do.'"**[170]

So the Prophet advised his followers to make good use of their abilities and of any excess time they find to increase their positive and constructive endeavors, saying, *"There are two blessings of which many people are deprived: health and free time."*[171] And he told them: *"Fear Allah wherever you are, and follow up a bad deed with a good one; it will erase it. And treat people with good manners."*[172] *"The best of people is one whose life is long and deeds are good, and the worst of people is one whose life is long and deeds are bad."*[173]

It was his duty to convey to people what kind of deeds are pleasing to Allah and to inform them that they must exert effort to prove their faith. That he did in the most complete manner. It remains for those who claim belief to confirm it, as Allah clearly stated that there is responsibility on both sides: **"Upon him [the Messenger] is only that with which he has been charged, and upon you is that with which you have been charged."**[174]

170Qur'an, 9:105.
171Narrated by al-Bukhari and at-Tirmidhi.
172Narrated by Ahmad, Abu Dawud and at-Tirmidhi – *hasan*.
173Narrated by Ahmad and at-Tirmidhi – *saheeh*.
174Qur'an, 24:54.

In order to do something in the most efficient and effective way, adequate knowledge of it is required. In particular, one must know the correct ways of securing Allah's approval and reward, as was confirmed and emphasized by His Messenger:

"Seeking knowledge is an obligation upon every Muslim."[175] *"Whoever follows a path seeking knowledge, Allah will facilitate for him a path to Paradise."*[176]

"He who follows a path in pursuit of knowledge – Allah will make easy for him a path to Paradise. The angels lower their wings for the seeker of knowledge, being pleased with what he does. The inhabitants of the heavens and the earth, even the fish in the depths of the oceans, ask forgiveness for him. The superiority of the learned person over the ritual worshipper is like that of the moon over other planets. The learned are heirs of the prophets; prophets leave neither dinars nor dirhams but only knowledge, and he who acquires it has in fact acquired an abundant share."[177]

"May Allah make radiant the face of a person who hears from me a statement and conveys it as he heard it. It might be that one who hears it understands better than the one who conveys it."[178] *"Whoever invites to right guidance will have reward equal to the rewards of all those who follow it without it lessening anything from their own rewards."*[179]

The Prophet always encouraged the pursuit and teaching of knowledge. This included insight into history, an understanding of the natural laws governing occurrences, development of the earth for the benefit of

---

[175]Narrated by al-Bayhaqi and at-Tabarani – *saheeh*.

[176]Narrated by Muslim.

[177]Narrated by Ahmad – *saheeh*. The *dinar* and *dirham* were the units of currency in use at the time.

[178]Ahmad and at-Tirmidhi – *saheeh*.

[179]Narrated by Ahmad and Muslim.

humanity, the need to refer to specialists in every field, regulation of public and private conduct, techniques of dialogue with discipline and diplomacy, awareness of actual realities, consideration of existing situations, perception of the aims behind legal rulings, and application of necessary conditions for acceptability of deeds.

According to the Qur'an and *sunnah,* there are two requirements for Allah's acceptance of any deed: 1) correctness, meaning that it is something lawful and done according to the way prescribed by Allah and His Messenger, and 2) sincerity, meaning that it is done for the approval of Allah alone. That is why the Prophet warned, *"Perhaps a fasting person gains nothing from his fast but hunger, and perhaps one who stands in night prayers gains nothing from his prayer but wakefulness."*[180] And, *"Anyone who innovates something in this religion of ours that is not a part of it – it will be rejected."*[181]

And some of the most significant and essential information regarding work and worship left by the Messenger is the following:

"The most beloved deeds to Allah are the most regular, even if they are few."[182] *"Take on from deeds whatever you are able, for Allah does not lose interest until you do. And indeed, the most beloved deeds to Allah are those that continue, even if they are few."*[183]

"Indeed, Allah has ordained conscientiousness in every matter."[184] *"Allah likes when one of you does something that he does it well."*[185] *"Allah likes when one of you does something that he does it with precision."*[186]

---

[180]Narrated by Ibn Majah – *saheeh.*

[181]Meaning that it will not be accepted by Allah. Narrated by al-Bukhari and Muslim.

[182]Narrated by al-Bukhari and Muslim.

[183]Narrated by al-Bukhari and Muslim.

[184]Narrated by Muslim.

[185]Narrated by at-Tabarani – *hasan.*

[186]Narrated by al-Bayhaqi – *hasan.*

"Allah, the Exalted, has said, 'I am the most self-sufficient, needing no partner. So whoever does a deed for Me and another [simultaneously], I abandon him and his partnership.'"[187]

"There must be no obedience to a created being in disobedience of the Creator."[188] *"Whoever seeks the acceptance of Allah but angering people – Allah will free him from dependence on people, and whoever seeks the acceptance of people by angering Allah – Allah will leave him to the people."*[189]

"When a servant becomes ill or travels, Allah, the Exalted, registers for him the same as he used to earn when he was well and at home."[190]

"One who asks Allah for martyrdom truthfully will reach the position of the martyrs even though he should die on his bed."[191]

"When a man dies, his deeds are ended except for three: a continuing charity, beneficial knowledge [left by him], and a righteous child who supplicates for him."[192]

Some of his companions asked the Prophet about the issue of predestination – whether there was any use in performing good deeds since Allah had already decreed who was destined for Hell and who was destined for Paradise. He answered, *"Work, for everyone is eased toward that for which he was created."* Then he recited to them: **"As for he who gives and fears Allah and believes in the best [reward], We will ease him toward ease. But as for he who withholds and considers himself free of need and denies the best [reward], We will ease him toward difficulty."**[193]

---

[187]Narrated by Muslim.

[188]Narrated by Ahmad and at-Tirmidhi – *saheeh*.

[189]Narrated by at-Tirmidhi – *saheeh*.

[190]Narrated by Ahmad and al-Bukhari.

[191]Narrated by Muslim.

[192]Narrated by Muslim.

[193]Narrated by al-Bukhari and Muslim. The Qur'anic verses are 92:5-10.

He meant that Allah decrees each person's destiny due to a cause, and that cause is his intent and action throughout his life on earth. Divine knowledge of what every individual will do during his life cannot affect his freedom to decide and act for himself, because he himself does not know what his Lord has decreed, and hence, he is entirely responsible for his own choice. When a person intends to do evil in spite of his Creator's guidance and warnings, Allah is displeased and leaves him to himself unless he repents and seeks forgiveness. And when someone intends to do what is right and good, Allah helps him to accomplish it and to earn its reward.

The Prophet encouraged people to think and to seek knowledge. He demonstrated how the unique characteristics of each individual should be capitalized upon and channeled in the right direction, alluding to this fact when he said: *"Everyone is eased toward that for which he was created."* He was speaking not only about Paradise and Hell but about the individual distinctions that need to be developed, refined and directed away from evil and toward the service of mankind.

He also established the principles and systematic methodology for obtaining knowledge, imparting it and acting upon it.[194] Tendencies toward excess among his companions were checked and corrected. Both fundamental and secondary issues were given due attention, as all are part of the religion, but fundamentals always took priority, for they are the base for all other reforms. Muslims were never allowed to become preoccupied with means and procedures to the point of forgetting their major objectives.

194This principle is evident in the Qur'an's revelation. Early verses dealt with the establishment of faith and motivation before introducing and imposing legislation. Obviously, a rational person will only accept a restriction or ruling when trusting in its benefit or in the wisdom of the lawmaker.

The *sunnah,* when understood and applied in an intelligent and balanced manner, puts all affairs in order, from personal and social etiquette to the politics of government and international relations. It is the key to everything good and desirable, the foundation of a superior civilization, and the path to success in the present life and the life to come.

The Prophet's Supplication – Muslims have always been encouraged to learn and recite some of the invocations that were taught or spoken by the Messenger of Allah, not only because his words are concise, comprehensive and linguistically eloquent but because obviously, he was the one most knowledgeable about how the Creator of the universe should be addressed. Of additional importance is the Prophet's manner when addressing his exalted Lord: his humbleness and sincerity, his acknowledgement of human imperfection, his gratitude for favors and blessings, his presence of mind and concentration, his urgency and polite persistence, and his trust in the wisdom and response of Allah. This too represents a significant feature of the *sunnah.*

When utilized correctly, supplication is an effective instrument for the acquisition of what is desired and prevention of what is feared. Information and instruction on this subject was offered by the Messenger of Allah: *"Nothing repels fate except supplication..."*[195] *"Whoever would like Allah to respond to him during hardship and disaster should supplicate much in times of ease."*[196]

"Three supplications are answered: the supplication of one who is fasting, the supplication of one who has been wronged, and the supplication of a traveler."[197] *"Three*

---

[195]Narrated by at-Tirmidhi and al-Hakim – *hasan.* This means that a destiny which might have been, had Allah not willed to prevent it, is changed by Him due to the supplication of His righteous servant (of which He had previous knowledge).

[196]Narrated by at-Tirmidhi – *hasan.*

[197]Narrated by al-Bayhaqi – *saheeh.*

supplications are answered without doubt: the supplication of one who has been wronged, the supplication of a traveler, and the supplication of a parent for his child."[198]

"Do not supplicate against yourselves and do not supplicate against your children and do not supplicate against your servants and do not supplicate against your properties."[199] *"Do not supplicate for death and do not wish for it. But whoever must, let him say, 'O Allah, give me life as long as life is best for me, and cause me to die when death is best for me.'"*[200]

It is evident, however, from both the Prophet's biography and the early history of Islam that the *sunnah* does not advocate supplication alone. Rather, it is required in conjunction with adequate effort based on sound knowledge. Both physical effort and supplication are causes and means of obtaining the desired effect in any endeavor, and neglect of either one will weaken the force that determines an outcome. For example, forgiveness of sin cannot be obtained except by repentance, regret and determination never again to return to the offense in addition to prolonged, sincere supplication to Allah for His forgiveness. And any project undertaken requires a sufficient amount of planning, preparation and hard work accompanied by supplication to Allah. Similarly, the perceptive believer seeks refuge in Allah from evil while doing his utmost to avoid it; and he asks Allah for Paradise while striving hard to attain it through righteous actions.

Allah's Messenger made maximum use of supplication as an essential supplement to his best efforts according to the law of cause and effect. His method was to strive hard while calling upon Allah for support and assistance,

---

[198]Narrated by Ibn Majah – *hasan*. These three are given by way of example, not limitation.
[199]Narrated by Muslim and Abu Dawud.
[200]Narrated by an-Nasa'i – *saheeh*.

since proper action and persistent supplication are among the most powerful causes of success. So he asked and worked, implored and labored; and then he was answered and aided.

From time to time, Allah tests the patience of His servants by prolonging difficult conditions. When nothing more can be done by a person to alter a situation, the aid of Allah should be sought through fervent supplication. One should never discontinue supplication thinking that response is slow or not forthcoming, for He will surely respond. Allah is pleased by continuing supplication which shows trust in Him; He rewards for it, provides psychological relief, and responds in the way which He knows will be best. As His Messenger explained:

"No Muslim supplicates to Allah with a supplication that is free from sin and from that which severs ties of relationship but that Allah will give him one of three things: a direct response to his supplication or the accumulation of its reward for him in the Hereafter or the prevention of an evil from striking him which is equal to it [i.e., to his effort in supplication]."[201]

He further disclosed, *"The closest a servant can be to his Lord is when he is prostrating [in prayer], so [at that time] supplicate abundantly."*[202] Though Allah is exalted and high above His creation, the Muslim draws nearest to Him by lowering his face to the ground in sincere worship and humble submission. At such a time his supplication is even more likely than usual to earn response.

The words of prophetic supplication obviously reflect the ideal relationship between a devout, dedicated man and his Creator. But they are much more than eloquent expression and moving sentiment. They reveal an inner dimension of the *sunnah* which provides guidance and direction for every person's life. What the Prophet

---

[201]Narrated by Ahmad – *hasan*.
[202]Narrated by Muslim.

requested from his Lord is everything meaningful, valuable and worthwhile in both the present life and that to come. In addition, he knew the subtle aspects of evil from which to seek protection from his Lord.

Allah's Messenger knew exactly what to ask for and how to ask for it. Examination of this element of the *sunnah* will reveal unmistakably what everyone should try to avoid because of its harm as well as the noble objectives that should be desired, sought after and worked for by every believer, in fact, by every human being on earth.

The Messenger of Allah identified these objectives and made them known to others through his own supplications, which were noted attentively by his companions, memorized and then taught as a part of the dynamic *sunnah* that went on to civilize the world. He would humbly praise and then address his Lord:

"O Allah, I am Your servant, the son of Your male servant and Your female servant. My forelock is in Your hand. Your decision is being carried out in me. Your decree on me is justice. I ask You by every name of Yours, which You have named Yourself or revealed in Your Book or taught any one of Your creation or kept within Your knowledge of the unseen, to make the magnificent Qur'an the revival of my heart, the illumination of my breast, the removal of my sadness, and the departure of my worry."[203]

"O Allah, forgive me, have mercy on me, guide me, grant me well-being and provide for me."[204] *"O Allah, set right my religion, which is the safeguard of my affairs; and set right my world, wherein is my livelihood; and set right my hereafter, to which is my return. And make life for me an increase in all good, and make death for me a relief from every evil."*[205]

---

[203]Narrated by Ahmad – *saheeh*.
[204]Narrated by at-Tirmidhi, Abu Dawud and Ibn Majah – *saheeh*.
[205]Narrated by Muslim.

"My Lord, assist me and assist not others against me. Grant me victory and grant not victory to others over me. Plan in favor of me and plan not for others against me. Guide me and make guidance easy for me; and aid me against whoever should oppress me. My Lord, make me one who continually remembers You, who is continually grateful to You, who continually fears You, who continually obeys You, continually praying and returning to You. My Lord, accept my repentance, remove my offense, respond to my supplication, establish my evidence, guide my heart, direct my tongue and eliminate resentment from my breast. O Allah, inspire me to sensible conduct and protect me from the evil of my soul."[206]

"O Allah, conceal my faults and remove my fears. O Allah, guard me from before me and behind me, on my right and on my left and above me. And I seek refuge in Your grandeur from being seized unaware from below."[207]

"O Allah, grant my soul consciousness [of You] and purify it, for You are the best to purify it. You are its protector and guardian."[208] *"O Allah, I seek refuge in You from laziness, decrepitude, debt and sin."*[209] *"O Allah, I ask You for guidance, righteousness, chastity and self-sufficiency."*[210]

"O Allah, I seek refuge in You from the evil of what I have done and from the evil of what I have not done."[211] *"O Allah, I seek refuge in You from the distress of trial, from the lowest level of misery, the perversity of fate, and the malicious rejoicing of enemies."*[212] *"O Allah, make not our misfortune in our religion and make not the world our greatest concern nor the sum of our knowledge."*[213]

---

[206]Narrated by Abu Dawud, at-Tirmidhi, an-Nasa'i and Ibn Majah – *saheeh*.
[207]Narrated by Abu Dawud – *hasan*.
[208]Narrated by Muslim.
[209]Narrated by Muslim.
[210]Narrated by Muslim and at-Tirmidhi.
[211]Narrated by Muslim.
[212]Narrated by al-Bukhari and Muslim.
[213]Narrated by at-Tirmidhi and al-Hakim – *saheeh*.

"O Allah, I seek refuge in You from knowledge that does not benefit, from a heart that is not humbled, from a soul that is not satisfied, and from supplication that is not answered. O Allah, I seek refuge in You from the cessation of Your favors, from a change in the well-being You have given me, from Your unexpected vengeance, and from all that angers You. O Allah, director of hearts, direct our hearts toward obedience to You."[214]

"O Allah, grant us a fear of You [sufficient] to prevent us from disobeying You, and obedience to You enabling us to reach Your Paradise, and the certainty which renders disasters of this world unimportant to us. O Allah, let us enjoy our hearing, our sight and our strength as long as You grant us life, and make it remaining among us. Make our vengeance upon those who oppress us and support us against our enemies. Let not our misfortune be in our religion and let not the world be our greatest concern or the limit of our knowledge. And do not empower over us those who show us no mercy."[215]

"O Allah, I seek refuge in You from bad manners, deeds, desires and diseases."[216]

"O Allah, I seek refuge in You from anxiety and grief, from failure and laziness, from cowardice and stinginess, from the constriction of debt and being overpowered by men. And I seek refuge in You from the torment of the grave and from the trials of life and death."[217]

"O Allah, I hope for Your mercy, so leave me not to myself for even the wink of an eye. And amend for me all of my affairs. There is no god but You."[218] "O Allah, make sufficient for me what You have permitted so I may avoid

---

214Narrated by Muslim.
215Narrated by at-Tirmidhi – *saheeh*.
216Narrated by at-Tirmidhi – *saheeh*.
217Narrated by al-Bukhari and Muslim.
218Narrated by Abu Dawud – *hasan*.

what You have prohibited; and make me self-sufficient by Your favor so I may need no one but You."[219]

"O Allah, forgive me what I have done and what I have delayed, what I concealed and what I revealed, the excess I have committed and that of which You are more knowing than me."[220] *"O Allah, forgive me my sin, all of it; the minute and the obvious of it, the first and the last of it, the apparent and the secret of it.*"[221]

"O Allah, I ask You for all goodness, what I know of it and what I do not know; and I seek refuge in You from all evil, what I know of it and what I do not know. O Allah, I ask You of Your favor and mercy, for none possesses them but You."[222] *"O Allah, I ask You for useful knowledge, for lawful sustenance, and for work acceptable to You."*[223] *"O Allah, I ask You to grant me the performance of good deeds and the abandonment of bad ones, love of the poor, and Your forgiveness and mercy. And if You intend a trial for people, let me die without having failed in trial."*[224]

"I seek refuge in Your approval from Your anger and in Your pardon from Your penalty. I seek refuge in You from You. I cannot adequately praise You; You are as You have praised Yourself."[225]

"O Allah, You created my soul and it is You who will take it; to You belongs its death and its life. O Allah, if You should keep it alive, then safeguard it; and if You should cause it to die, then forgive it. O Allah, I ask You for freedom from all evil."[226] *"O Allah, make the best of my*

---

[219]Narrated by at-Tirmidhi – *hasan*.
[220]Narrated by al-Bukhari and Muslim.
[221]Narrated by Muslim.
[222]Narrated by at-Tabarani – *saheeh*.
[223]Ibn Majah – *hasan*.
[224]Narrated by al-Bazzar – *hasan*.
[225]Narrated by Muslim.
[226]Narrated by Muslim.

days the Day when I meet You, the best of my life the last of it, and the best of my deeds the final ones."[227]

These are but a few of the supplications that offer a glimpse into the heart of the final Prophet and reflect his aspirations for his followers and their future generations. Like all other prophets he was a human being, and despite his extraordinary accomplishments, never claimed divine status. He called people to the worship of God alone, and insisted they refer to him as "Allah's servant and messenger." Through obedience and selflessness, effort and reliance on Allah, he and his companions built a society based upon principles of strong faith and morality combined with those of material progress – one unequaled in the history of mankind.

CONCLUSION

Allah, the Exalted, stated clearly in the Qur'an that this world, along with the present universe, will one day come to an end in order to make way for the new creation in which balance and justice prevail. Its final era began with the prophethood of Muhammad and will close at the Hour of Resurrection. There will be no divine scripture after the Qur'an and no prophet after Muhammad. He once observed, *"I and the Final Hour are like these two,"* and held up his index and middle fingers.[228]

The Prophet's *sunnah* is second only to the Qur'an as a source of Islamic legislation, and both are indispensable. He said, *"I have indeed been given the Qur'an and with it what is similar to it. Yet, a time will come when someone reclining on his couch will say, 'Follow only the Qur'an; take as permissible what you find in it as permissible, and take as prohibited what you find in it as prohibited.' But indeed, what the Messenger forbids is the same as what*

---

[227]Narrated by al-Bukhari and Muslim.
[228]Narrated by al-Bukhari and Muslim.

Allah has forbidden."[229]   The Qur'an itself confirms: **"Whoever obeys the Messenger has obeyed Allah."**[230]

The *sunnah* remains with us as the divinely ordained supplement to the Qur'an.   It contains a diversity of options for various situations and conditions present in the world at any given time and place.   It imparts the most effective methods of accomplishment which demand a conscious awareness of the priorities of each day and every hour.   Within the vast range of righteous deeds derived from the *sunnah,* a Muslim finds what is compatible with the needs of his particular society and with his own capacity for service.   Thus, he is not limited to forms of private worship but also actively participates in every lawful field of life, excelling in production, precision, skill and integrity, all the while earning the reward of a sincere worshipper.   And at the same time, he becomes a source of benefit and blessing within his community.

Prophet Muhammad was chosen by the Creator of the universe and mankind to invite all people to the correct beliefs and pure way of life preferred by Him and to demonstrate the measures and methods leading to His acceptance.   He spared no effort and no sacrifice in carrying out this duty for the benefit of mankind. Through him, God made known truth from falsehood and wisdom from error.   And through him He showed man how to attain eternal Paradise.

What was taught by Prophet Muhammad is as fundamental today as ever before.   The *sunnah* provides the means to achieve the noble existence for which Allah created human beings.   The straight path to which the Prophet invited by word and deed is, simply stated, the shortest route to true and lasting contentment.   It is the path leading to a satisfying relationship with the Creator

---

229Narrated by Ahmad and Abu Dawud – *saheeh*.
230Qur'an, 4:80.

of mankind and to His unlimited mercy, appreciation and generosity. It is a median path of moderation and reason, avoiding every form of excess or extremism. It is a path based upon honesty and sincere effort in the present world which ultimately leads to full compensation and perfect justice in the next.

Islam is a complete way of life, combining aspects of faith and worship, legislation and moral teachings to offer the most intensive and effective means to purify and refine the human soul and human societies. Unlike many other religions and ideologies which emphasize some aspects of man's nature at the expense of others, Islam does justice to the demands of all three of his faculties: the physical, intellectual and spiritual. Among its unique features are the following:

- Islam is the only religion whose sources are authentically preserved and have remained immaculately free of human alteration and interference.

- Its divine scripture, the Qur'an, is free of mythical elements incompatible with modern man's understanding of the world. It is in harmony with the established facts of science, clearly bearing the signature of the author of the universe.

- The Qur'an provides answers to questions that haunt the mind of every intelligent person, those related to the purpose of life and about further existence after death. In it one will find:

1. Information about the Creator, in particular His perfect and absolute attributes
2. The purpose of creation and of life on earth
3. The way one should relate to his Creator, to his fellow men, and to the universe in general
4. Disclosure of one's final return to his Creator for evaluation and the consequences of his attitudes and behavior

- The Qur'an upholds the role of the mind and regards those who fail to use reason as intellectually deficient. This is distinct from the teachings of many religions which assume the incompatibility of faith and reason. The Qur'an is unique in its approach to knowledge, stressing observation, experience and intellect rather than custom and blind assumption.

- Islamic beliefs and practices are natural and appeal to common sense. They take into account both the instincts and faculties of human beings and present a balanced program of life that caters to basic physical as well as spiritual needs. Additionally, Islam provides an ideal role model in the person of Prophet Muhammad, whose biography, unlike great heroes and founders of other religions, has been recorded in minute detail and is easily accessible for study. Islamic history has also provided the example of a model society where truth and transparency, justice, and compassion were actually implemented and maintained as a vital expression of the religion.

- Islam stresses human brotherhood, eliminating the negative consequences of tribalism, nationalism and racism which create and sustain conflicts.

- Islam is the only religion which insists upon worship of the Creator alone and completely rejects the worship of any of His creations. Hence, it provides liberation from servitude to other men as well as the highest spiritual fulfillment and contentment that humans are capable of attaining.

- Islam dispenses with all intermediaries between man and God and allows all humans to contact Him directly, thus eliminating hierarchies and other sources of religious exploitation which have characterized religious history throughout the ages.

The Messenger of Allah was sent to mankind with complete guidance in all matters of faith and its application to the affairs of human life in order that everyone might attain the happiness and contentment of this world and the next. By following the guidance found in the Qur'an and *sunnah,* man can fully experience his human worth and his special position among created beings. And by so doing, he will automatically come into harmony with the rest of creation, earn the approval of his Lord, and obtain peace and contentment in a better and permanent existence to come.

All praise is due to Allah, and may His blessings and peace be upon Muhammad, the last of the prophets, and upon his companions and all those who follow his guidance until the Day of Recompense.

REFERENCES

al-Albani, Muhammad Nasiruddeen, *Saheeh al-Jami' as-Sagheer*, Beirut: al-Maktab al-Islami, 1988.

al-Albani, Muhammad Nasiruddeen, *Silsilah al-Ahadeeth as-Saheehah*, Riyadh: Maktabat al-Ma'aarif, 1995.

al-'Asqalani, Ibn Hajar, *Fath al-Bari bi Sharh Saheeh al-Bukhari*, Beirut: Dar al-Ma'rifah, 1970.

Hamidullah, Muhammad, *Introduction to Islam*, Paris: Centre Culturel Islamique, 1969.

Ibn al-Qayyim, Muhammad, *Zad al-Ma'ad*, Beirut: Mu'assassat ar-Risalah, 1985.

Ibn Hisham, 'Abdul-Malik, *As-Seerah an-Nabawiyyah*, Cairo: Maktabat Mustafa al-Babi al-Halabi, 1955.

Kazi, Mazhar U., *Self-Evident Miracles of the Holy Qur'an*, Jeddah: Abul-Qasim Publishing House, 1998.

al-Mubarakpuri, Safiur Rahman, *Ar-Raheeq al-Makhtum*, Riyadh: Dar-us-Salam, 1996.

an-Nawawi, Yahya Sharaf, *Saheeh Muslim bi Sharh an-Nawawi*, Cairo: Dar ar-Rayan lit-Turath, 1987.

al-Qahtaani, Sa'eed bin 'Ali, *Hisnul-Muslim*, Riyadh: Ministry of Islamic Affairs, Waqf, Da'wah and Guidance, 1420 H.

al-Qaradawi, Yusuf, *Islamic Awakening Between Rejection and Extremism*, Herndon, USA: International Institute of Islamic Thought, 1995.

al-Qaradawi, Yusuf, *The Sunnah: A Source of Civilization*, Cairo: El-Falah, 1998.

Saheeh International, *The Qur'an – Arabic Text with Corresponding English Meanings*, Jeddah: Abul-Qasim Publishing House, 1997.

Sharafuddeen, Siddiqah, *The Muslim's Supplication*, Jeddah: Abul-Qasim Publishing House, 1994.

al-Umari, Akram Diya, *Madinan Society at the Time of the Prophet*, Herndon, USA: International Institute of Islamic Thought, 1995.

al-Umari, Akram Diya, *As-Seerah an-Nabawiyyah as-Saheehah*, Madinah: Maktabat al-'Uloom wal-Hikam, 1994.

Umm Muhammad, *The Prophets Appointed by Allah*, Jeddah: Abul-Qasim Publishing House, 1992.